Pra

RISE ABOVE
DEPRESSION

"As a professional speaker, I know every audience member craves the answer to three questions: Why should I listen to you? (Credibility) Can I do it too? (Possibility) What do I do next? (Usability). *Rise Above Depression* is an inspirational masterpiece that not only answers these questions, but also reminds us that failure is an event, not a person. The authors acknowledge what it's like to be wounded and hurting, but show that being "Present In Every Moment" we can realize that adversity introduces us to our real selves, and that depression is an injury from which we can recover and heal."

— Dan Clark, Hall of Fame Speaker, New York Times Best Selling Author

"Jodi's book offers hope to every one suffering from not only depression, but any sort of mental or physical 'paralysis.' Her messages of hope versus hopelessness inspired me so much that I've sent the book to others I know who struggle with issues, physical, mental and spiritual. Reading this book proves a person can overcome anything, no excuses. I appreciate the inspiring stories of others who have found themselves in the face of adversity and have been able to move forward with faith and a positive outlook on life."

— Chad Hymas, Author of *Doing What Must Be Done,* Hall of Fame Speaker

"The powerful truth that we are much, much more than our bodies is only the beginning of what Jodi Orgill Brown expounds on in this must-read book. Discover keys on how to not only deal with, but overcome the things which in the end make us magnificent. An inspirational page-turner in developing trust and tenacity as we 'press on' with the challenges in our lives."

— Jeffery Olsen, Co-Founder @ONE, Best Selling Author

"Since most of us will either experience depression ourselves or be close to someone who does, it is important that we begin to understand the difficult challenges of those affected by this disease. In 'Rise Above Depression,' the authors have created a work that is accessible to everyone and provides valuable insights and tools to deal with this very serious illness. Jodi Orgill Brown has done a masterful job of exploring this topic through the voices of many who are suffering. Each of their experiences is unique, and yet they all provide encouragement and hope for a better life. This is one of those books that will literally change lives."

— Steve Ostler, CEO, One Refugee

"When I first started the book, I thought I was reading to understand and learn more about how I could understand and help those that deal with depression. I soon realized this book is not just for those who suffer from the effects of depression, but it's also for any person looking live a fuller, more purposeful life. This book is filled with simple daily tools and stories you could apply to life regardless of depression.

It took me through a personal journey of looking how I can better my life and help create more joy for others. I would recommend this book to ALL who want to make a profound difference in their own life and make an impact on other peoples' lives, regardless of whether or not you suffer from depression. This book is truly an inspired book and will continue to make a big impact in the world as it is shared and spread."

— Andrea Tesch, Mother, Speaker, Entrepreneur

"Someone once said, regarding their search for inner peace, 'In the depth of winter, I finally learned that within me there lay an invincible summer' *(Albert Camus)*. Jodi Orgill Brown has created and compiled precious principles, insights, and wisdom that will bless anyone suffering from depression, anxiety or emotional trauma, with crucial guides and directions to help find their 'invincible summer.' The darkness and despair of depression are dispelled enough for us to take action. From there we can see an end to, or at least a viable way to endure and even find joy in, our suffering. The experiences, insights and counsel—shared with intense personal empathy—provide many of these key anchors of hope and can guide us to summer."

— John Paskett, VP of Operations, Personal Strengths Publishing, PTSD Survivor, and father of eight

Maggie,
With perspective, you can always

RISE ABOVE
DEPRESSION

ENCOURAGEMENT AND TIPS FROM THOSE WHO DO IT
EVERY DAY

JODI ORGILL BROWN

Award-Winning Author of *The Sun Still Shines*

Fulfill
Publishing

Fulfill
Publishing

Author Photo by: Rusty Sessions, Sidewinder Media
Cover image by: Axel Lauerer
Cover design by: Andee Hales Sanders

Email: www.jod@jodiobrown.com
Instagram: jodiorgillbrown
Facebook: www.facebook.com/writerjodibrown

Read the AUTHOR'S award-winning book:

The Sun Still Shines

Book JODI ORGILL BROWN to speak at an event:

www.JodiOBrown.com

BONUS! Download FREE happiness guide at:
http://bit.ly/riseabovedepression

TABLE OF CONTENTS

Part III: Personal Essays of Strength During the Rise

RISE ABOVE **DEPRESSION**

* By request, some names have been changed to protect the privacy of the individuals.

** Jodi Orgill Brown authors all sections and chapters not otherwise attributed to an individual author.

For Kristi and Brandon

FOREWORD:

WHY RISE ABOVE

Depression is not necessarily something that can always be OVERCOME. Unlike certain medical conditions that, once treated, depart permanently, depression has multiple triggers with correlating brain and body conditions, which must be regularly addressed. Nearly every one of the seven billion people on the planet will experience depressive episodes at some time.

To RISE ABOVE does not guarantee an end to suffering; it means you PRESS ON with a new perspective, one that can offer hope and possibility.

Seeing from an airplane viewpoint causes obstacles, even mountains which seemed insurmountable, to decrease in size or disappear from view. Borders and boundaries blend into the background. Landmasses merge as one. When you rise, you don't lose the ability to see things closely; instead, you gain the ability to see things in a new way. Then you can find a route around the blockades that trap your mind and body.

PRESS ON

I didn't choose to write this book. The call to complete this project came from a higher power—and after some hesitation, I accepted the invitation.

The idea came to me when I was in the car, traveling with my family. The serious effects of depression weighed heavily on my mind. Too many people I love battle with depression, and sometimes, the demon wins. My personal experiences with battling depression, following complications from a brain tumor, had once left me questioning my own purpose and life. Though I had no specific answer, I realized something more needed to be done.

In that moment, the universe presented me with an opportunity. I wanted to say, "No", but the pull was too strong.

The moment of agreement occurred quietly in the car. With a sigh of acceptance came a thought, one never voiced out loud. "Well, if I am going to do this, what is it supposed to look like?"

No sooner did I pose the question than I envisioned an image. I grabbed a sticky note and drew an illustration of the word as I saw it in my mind. Similar to the typographic representation of the word DEPRESSION on the cover of the book, I saw the answer, once concealed, suddenly appear: Press On.

Immediately I knew this was bigger than a project or a book; it was an invitation to the sufferers in the world to share their stories, to press on, and to rise above depression.

COURAGE TO RISE ABOVE

"What makes us vulnerable makes us beautiful."
-- Dr. Brené Brown, New York Times bestselling author & researcher

The ultimate goal of *Rise Above Depression* is to help readers find their individual paths to healing from depression.

The *Rise Above Depression* team believes all people can have and deserve a life of happiness, and our choices contribute to help us either actualize joy or permit misery. The book provides tools to control what we can control—our thoughts and actions—and to make incremental steps from depression to authentic, present, in-the-moment happiness.

Whole healing from depression requires a tailored and multi-faceted approach that is unique to each person; therefore, this book provides a range of perspectives and experiences which readers can draw upon for basic scientific understanding and real-world implementation.

Note: This book is not a one-size-fits-all solution to the struggle of depression, nor is it a minimization of the serious health, physical, and life challenges that contribute to depression. This book does not include a full explanation of depression research, or experiences of depression, nor is it a substitute for medical intervention, professional counseling, medication, or therapy.

HOW TO USE THIS BOOK

Each chapter in *Rise Above Depression* features comments from real sufferers of depression. Sixteen individuals authored chapters or major sections, and more than 50 individuals contributed stories, essays, tips, suggestions, and hard-to-relive moments that are woven throughout this book. The styles, points of view, and narratives are their own, written to help you.

Though many of the contributors have suffered tirelessly from the effects of depression, including attempted suicide, the *hells* of their journeys are not the focus of this book. With exceptions in three chapters, suicide is not a prominent topic in the text. Neither is addiction, which is often a precursor to suicide attempts, a prominent topic. Suicide and addiction are preventable tragedies. Both problems provoke the need to deal with depression as a major societal issue—and as a private, individual issue.

All contributions are shared with the intent to provide hope and answers, not to further immerse readers in the depths of suffering.

The goals of this publication are to help readers:

- Know that you are not alone.
- Find understanding and hope for a better future.
- Discover ideas and tools that will work to heal YOU.

Read Chapter 1, "A Place in the Tribe". Then choose your own path.

- If you are interested in HOW your brain works so you can understand WHY the stories and suggestions will help your mental health, then read Part I.
- If you are flailing or drowning right now, then go to Part II. Peruse the chapters to discover a topic that resonates with you, and then read the chapter. Or, go to the last page of each chapter and read the "Quick Can-Do Tips."
- If you are stalled in your daily fight to PRESS ON, then go to Part III and read the personal essays detailing the experiences and lessons others have learned on their journeys. Find similarities, differences, will-tries, and hope—so you, too, can rise above.

PART I

THE MOODY CLUES IN THE BODY AND BRAIN

These chapters focus on the basic science and research for why we suffer from depression and the personal deceptions of depression. The research establishes a basis for understanding why the experiences, suggestions, tools, and tips in the rest of the book are worthy of trying.

CHAPTER 1:
A Place in the Tribe

by Angie Fenimore

Dawn is creeping over the mountain range, finally ending a particularly dark night. It's been several hours now since I received the text from Terri.

"Have you heard about Heather?"

Terri and I have bonded like sisters. But then, she is part of our tribe, the group of acquisition editors, literary agents, and the authors who serve on the faculty of Calliope Writing Coach, which my husband, Michael, and I run together. They, along with the hundreds of students that go through our program, become our family. And they all bond with each other.

Michael opens every course with this: "If you are nervous, if you didn't do anything to prepare for the course, if you haven't written a thing, don't worry. We've got you. By the time we wrap in three days, we will be family."

And we are. Three days is just the beginning of our time together. But this tribe of ours forms something more authentic and deeper than what many families know. To write is to express that which is most raw, most real within us. Our masks fall away, our dreams and our sadnesses can often only be spoken aloud to other writers, to other members of our tribe.

We have students that show up at our house to write all day, for support through a devastating break-up, or to share their triumphs. They hardly ever bother to knock on the door. They know we are family. We have two cats that once belonged to students. We've even moved a student in for several months who was evicted when his roommate was in a bicycle accident, laid up in the hospital, and couldn't pay his half of the rent. Our children tease that we should hang a sign over the threshold of our home that reads, "Humane Society." We laugh, because it's true.

The message came when Michael and I were enjoying a patio dinner at a local restaurant, soaking in the evening warmth after running back-to-back webinars for two days straight. I hadn't had a full minute to breathe, to call my sister to wish her a happy birthday, or to reach out to Heather, who was MIA in our new writers' program. I was dialing my sister's number when the message from Terri popped up on my screen. Then, that knot, that familiar empty feeling filled my gut, followed by the thoughts that always come when I suspect I'm being prepped for disturbing news.

"Which Heather?" I responded. I could think of at least three Heathers that Terri and I know in common. When she didn't immediately respond, I checked all the Facebook pages of all the Heathers who belong to our ever-expanding circle. Our editor friend might be expecting another baby, I thought. There's the Heather who supported me in bringing Calliope Writing Coach to fruition. We've been close friends for years. It was old news that she had moved to Canada.

And there was Heather Beachell. Michael and I had known her for a decade when she took one of our writing courses several months earlier. While Terri had only known her for a short time, they had shared rides and even discussed sharing an apartment together. Heather didn't hide her battle with depression and mental illness. She proudly voiced her passion, her calling to write her story, to take on the social stigmas associated with mental illness, and to embrace her own mental and emotional health. I wasn't sure if her particular afflictions were genetic, but I knew that she was estranged from her family, and that her heart ached over the state of her relationship with her mother.

I checked texts that I had exchanged with Heather. Our last

communication was two weeks earlier. She was excited about having been given a computer, so she could write. And she apologized that she was late with payments for her course. I reassured her that it was no big deal and that I was excited for her progress. She had an important message to share.

I messaged others who knew her well, fishing for more information. Word finally came. Heather had overdosed and was discovered days later by another friend. There was nothing on Facebook. No obituary. It finally came out that Heather's family was not holding a memorial service. Shiralee, the woman who'd opened her home to Heather and had discovered the tragedy, together with Michael and Terri and a few other members of our tribe, gathered in our home. We pieced together the timeline of events.

There were pieces of the puzzle that I knew, but Shiralee and Terri had the full backstory. Heather's living situation had become increasingly problematic. It began when her landlord shut off the air-conditioning and the water heater before taking an extended vacation, leaving Heather in a sweltering house for weeks. And then there were the odd rules. Don't use the kitchen after six o'clock. And no visitors. Friends who had offered Heather rides were not to drop her off in front of the house, but around the corner so as not to alert neighbors that Heather was renting a room in the home. We all knew that Heather was desperately trying to work out new living arrangements.

A physical altercation between Heather and the landlord had ended with an overnight stay in the hospital for Heather. The police took the landlord's statement before Heather told them her side of the story. She was then served with an eviction notice, and false charges were filed against her. To add to the trauma, a man she'd been dating had apparently lost interest and wasn't returning her calls.

Shiralee was headed to the coast for several days. She had offered her home, the refrigerator stocked with fresh vegetables and fruit, as well as the use of her car, all with the promise that they would sort out Heather's dilemma upon Shiralee's return. They spoke on the phone several times over the next few days. Heather appeared empowered, ready to navigate through the setback. We can't be certain whether it was Shiralee's last phone conversation with Heather, the apology that she penned and left on Shiralee's nightstand, or the last text that Terri received that was Heather's final communication.

"I don't know who to turn to," the text read. Terri's encouraging responses went unanswered. It's only in hindsight that we often comprehend the intentions behind the words.

THE NEED TO BELONG

From the cradle, the experience of "belonging" is a human need. Low birth-weight newborns do far better when they are held skin to skin with another human being. Psychology, sociology, and other fields of study have examined lack of human connection, lack of affection at great length.

No findings have left me as unsettled and heartbroken as the work that was done a decade after the Romanian orphan crisis came to light in 1989. When communism in that country fell and dictator Nikolae Ceausescu was overthrown, state-run orphanages with over 150,000 children were discovered. In many cases, these children received basic care, as in proper nutrition and diapering, but in some of the more rural orphanages, children were found to have been chained to their cribs…for years. For the most part, their physical needs were managed, except for one. They were deprived of physical contact. "Breathtakingly awful" was how Charles Nelson, professor of pediatrics at Harvard Medical School, described scene after scene.

The study covered six Bucharest orphanages and included a foster care system that was implemented for some of the children. Not surprisingly, the American Psychological Association reported that the lack of stimulation and lack of connection to a primary caregiver resulted in a multitude of maladies. The children experienced dissociative disorder, failure to thrive, and delays in motor development. Cognitive and language function were impaired. They exhibited deficits in socio-emotional behaviors and displayed psychiatric disorders. Even brain growth was diminished.

For the children who were placed into foster care, their futures were brighter, in particular if they were placed in a home by the age of two. These children were shown to form secure attachment relationships with their caregivers and made dramatic gains in their ability to express emotions. While they began to catch up with their peer groups in physical growth, and over time restored some of their missing brain matter volume, parts of their brains never recovered.

In short, the experience of connecting and belonging is clearly a human need. Even children raised in emotionally healthy environments continue to experience the need to belong. As we grow, go to school and expand our social environments, we begin to establish roles that we assume within our groups or tribes. We find our place. We experience belonging. Facing banishment and shame trigger greater fear responses in our brains than does impending death.

Staggering suicide rates among teens over "banishment" from their tribes at school is evidence enough that the need to survive within the tribe is alive and well. Suicide rates are climbing among our soldiers and veterans, as well as the elderly. There are strong links between a variety of mental illnesses and suicidal ideations. Even so, in my experience as an author committed to suicide prevention after surviving my own suicide attempt half my life ago, and in publicly addressing depression, what I've discovered over the last twenty-five years is that most people experience times when that line between choosing life and opting out is a fragile, worn thread.

There are tools I've developed, that I teach others, and that I practice myself that can provide relief from disempowering thoughts, including suicidal ideations. When I separate out my emotions, my physical experience, and my thoughts from the actual circumstances that I'm dealing with, I can see clearly. When I identify the emotions that accompany self-deprecating thoughts, I can locate those emotions in my earliest childhood memories of experiencing fear, of being a failure, of confusion, or of feeling abandoned. Then I can also see that as a child, those emotions were a fit for my accompanying experience, but that they are actually ghost emotions attached to an experience that is no longer impacting me. Those emotions no longer serve me. I can then relate to my disempowering thoughts rationally. Rather than entertain those thoughts and emotions or resist them, I allow them to pass through me.

I've also created a pact with my sister. We inherited depression disorder from our father. We reach out to each other when darkness and despair creep in. For some people, medication is part of an answer.

In Heather's case, what I'm asking myself as I sit in the darkness grieving the loss of a friend—a friend who belonged to my tribe—is this: What could I have said that I didn't? What didn't I do that might have made a difference? These are the question we are all haunted by in wake of losing a loved one to suicide. The answer lies within the question itself.

Heather did have a loving, supportive, devoted tribe. She did belong. She may have lost her birth family along the way, in particular, her mother, but she did have many friends who loved her, cared deeply for her, and would have supported her had they known that she was at the edge of what she could bare. Shiralee had shared Heather's burdens and supported her through many crises. She was a patient, listening friend to the end of Heather's life. There was a support system in place. But belief is more powerful than fact.

What was missing for Heather was clear in her final words to Terri, to all of us. "I don't know who to turn to." In addition to everything else she was dealing with, if even for a few hours, Heather believed that she didn't belong, that her life didn't matter. When we unwind the tangled "yarn" of that story we tell ourselves, what we find at the core is that we must *believe* that we belong. That *we exist* matters to someone else is fundamental to our happiness, our health, and sometimes, even to our desire to live.

Humane Society. A society built on the ideals that represent the best of who we are—based on the belief that every human life matters—this is my credo. I speak now to you, my friends who share this planet with me, who I may never meet while we walk the Earth together. If you have the experience that you are alone, search out a tribe. Create a pact with someone else. Promise that you will call, you will text, that you will reach out when you are so low that you must rely on a single strand of connection with another human being.

Allow disempowering thoughts to pass through you. Your thoughts do not originate within you. They do not belong to you. They do not own you. If you feel that you are alone, or that nobody cares, create a tribe. Service to others is the Balm of Gilead. We cannot help but love those whom we serve. Go to the local homeless shelter. Provide haircuts. Serve in the kitchen. Join a support group. And write your story. When you purge that which is trapped within you, you create an environment within yourself for healing. By serving, by writing, and by allowing disempowering thoughts to pass through you, you create room within yourself for light to expand. We must empty the vessel to receive.

As Mahatma Gandhi said, "The best way to find yourself is to lose yourself in the service of others."

And finally, to Heather. Godspeed, my friend. You, and your life mattered. You mattered to me.

In Memory of Heather Lynn Beachell

January 13, 1970 - August 29, 2017

About the Author: Angie Fenimore is an international bestselling author and writing coach. Read more from Angie in Chapter 4 and in Chapter 11. Find her online at www.angiefenimore.com.

CHAPTER 2:
To Heal the Whole

Heather Beachell is the answer for the question: WHY do we need this book? Her life, and the other 44,192 lives that will be lost to suicide in 2017, testifies of the need for action against depression.

In fact, the suicide rate in the United States has been steadily increasing since 1999, and the pace of the increase is climbing.

You are likely not consumed with the statistics of suicide or the science of depression. You are more likely consumed by how you feel. How IT makes you feel (see chapter 3). But the more you know about your opponent, the better your strategy for healing.

Active—if not aggressive—force is required for the caterpillar-cocoon-butterfly process of transformation that will take us from depression to whole healing. To inch forward, we need to learn how to evolve and then move in incremental steps.

Passivity does not empower change.

The chemical and physiological processes involved in depression and happiness are complex, but obtaining basic information enables activity. With education, you can become one of the planners for your custom-made transformation strategy.

The first step for healing is to understand the science of the body and mind to discern which treatments might work for you, and why. You know things about your body and experiences that your doctor, therapist, and test results may never uncover. Additionally, you know what and how you think and how you feel. To let others decide treatment without knowing all the facts is a path to frustration. And to engage in treatment without knowing why the treatment could work is a "take-this-pill" solution without knowing what you are ingesting.

The plans for your metamorphosis will involve multiple methods and individuals. They will likely require help from experts, doctors, therapists, wellness professionals, spiritual counselors, or social workers, as well as concerned family and friends. They may involve medication, mindfulness, social pacts, various self-help tools, and emergency numbers, but it is worth investing in help—for yourself, or for your loved one with depression.

HOLE VERSUS WHOLE

Healing the whole is more than not being depressed; it is healing the mind, freeing it to allow conscious focus on all other areas of wellbeing.

©Jodi Orgill Brown & Fulfill Publishing

Mental wellbeing is at the center of whole healing, but a powerful physical component accompanies it. Our bodies and minds comprise parts of a functioning human unit, not just conditions of that unit, and therefore they work together. Action, utilizing the physical body, reinforces the decisions we make mentally. Thus, both need to work in conjunction to turn the wheel of whole healing.

WHAT IS DEPRESSION?

CLINICAL DEPRESSION

Clinical depression, or major depressive disorder, is diagnosed when individuals exhibit five or more of the following symptoms within the same two-week period of time (from The Diagnostic and Statistical Manual of Mental Disorders by the American Psychiatric Association, or DSM-5):

1. Depressed mood most of the day, nearly every day, as indicated by either subjective report (e.g., feels sad, empty, hopeless) or observation made by others (e.g., appears tearful). (Note: In children and adolescents, can be irritable mood.)
2. Markedly diminished interest or pleasure in all, or almost all, activities most of the day, nearly every day (as indicated by either subjective account or observation.)
3. Significant weight loss when not dieting, or weight gain (e.g., a change of more than 5% of body weight in a month), or decrease or increase in appetite nearly every day. (Note: In children, consider failure to make expected weight gain.)
4. Insomnia or hypersomnia nearly every day.
5. Psychomotor agitation or retardation nearly every day (observable by others, not merely subjective feelings of restlessness or being slowed down).
6. Fatigue or loss of energy nearly every day.
7. Feelings of worthlessness or excessive or inappropriate guilt (which may be delusional) nearly every day (not merely self-reproach or guilt about being sick).
8. Diminished ability to think or concentrate, or indecisiveness, nearly every day (either by subjective

account or as observed by others).

9. Recurrent thoughts of death (not just fear of dying), recurrent suicidal ideation without a specific plan, or a suicide attempt or a specific plan for committing suicide.

The DSM-5 is also used to diagnose other kinds of depressive and mental disorders. (For example, it includes the diagnosis for post-traumatic stress disorder, which might overlap with major depressive disorder, but will not be identical.)

SITUATIONAL DEPRESSION

Trauma, transition, body chemistry, season changes, hormones, illness, environmental changes, or a life struggle can trigger a *case* of depression. Losing a loved one, being fired, having financial troubles, or major change of any kind can have serious effects. Every independent person will likely suffer situational depression at some time as life unfolds.

CONTRIBUTING RISK FACTORS

Many factors can increase your risk of developing situational or clinical depression at some point in life. However, risk factors are *not* direct causes of, nor guarantees, that an individual will suffer depression. These circumstances may contribute to depression, likely because they affect the natural production and release of the chemicals, hormones, and processes that regulate mood.

Risk factors are higher for individuals with the following scenarios:[ii]

- serious or chronic illness (cancer, brain trauma, or heart disease)
- degenerative neurological conditions, such as Parkinson's disease, Alzheimer's, Huntington's, or multiple sclerosis
- stroke
- childhood loss
- trauma or PTSD
- insomnia
- hormonal changes, including from pregnancy, childbirth, thyroid issues (hyperthyroidism and hypothyroidism), PMS,

menopause
- immune diseases and disorders, such as lupus
- low self-esteem
- blood relatives with depression
- infections and viruses, such as HIV, hepatitis, or mononucleosis
- mental disorders, such as anxiety or bipolar disorder
- gay, lesbian, bisexual, or transgender identities
- drug or alcohol use or abuse
- erectile dysfunction in men
- use of certain medications, like steroids, birth control pills, blood pressure pills, or sleeping pills[ii]
- limited exposure to sunlight, geographically or seasonally, (which is required for the body to make vitamin D)
- nutritional deficiencies, such as lack of vitamin B12

The research on the believed causes and contributors to depression amount to multiple volumes of information. Contributing factors are so various that there appears to be little correlation between some of the conditions, except that they are all related to changes in the *normal* functioning of the body.

Aye, there's the rub![iii] Is any *body* truly normal? Is it possible, or even desirable, to get through life without loss, illness, trauma, or stress? Perhaps life navigation requires occasional detours, slowdowns, and orange warning signs.

THE SCIENCE BEHIND
DEPRESSION AND TREATMENT

by Jessica Thornton

What is happening within your brain during a depressive episode? Changes within the brain during depression can be seen in brain scans and noted in behavioral and emotional changes. Research makes it difficult to determine whether these changes cause or are caused by depression, so the most we can say for sure is that the two are highly positively correlated. Some of the changes include

20

the following[iv]:

> *The hippocampus shrinks.* The hippocampus is responsible for memory and emotion formation. The shrinking of the hippocampus causes problems associated with the formation of new memories. The same effect can be seen in the prefrontal cortex, the brain's center for regulating emotion and decision-making.
>
> *Cortisol increases.* Cortisol, a hormone that is released when the mind or body is in distress, is primarily produced and controlled by the hippocampus. Changes in the hippocampus can affect production of cortisol, often releasing larger than normal amounts of the hormone.
>
> *The amygdala becomes overactive.* The amygdala, another source of emotion control, becomes overactive in response to high cortisol levels and causes disruptions of sleep cycles.
>
> *Serotonin decreases.* The brain's lack of the neurotransmitter serotonin causes a deficiency that also disrupts sleep patterns, as well as destabilizes emotions and mood.

These physiological changes upset the body's natural state, putting sufferers at risk for increased physical, mental, and emotional complications.

Modern treatments aim to reverse or slow the effects depression has on the brain, thus helping the patient recover. This is based on the premise of brain plasticity, or your brain's ability to change and adapt structurally. Certain structures within your brain can change in response to long-term exposure to stimuli, like exposure to cortisol as described above. A core tenet of modern treatments of depression is that by changing stimuli or behavior, the same structures in your brain can change back.

The coping mechanisms therapists recommend have the goal of stopping these effects by slowing cortisol production, or rebuilding and repairing neural pathways and brain cells. Cognitive behavioral therapy alters patterns of behavior, an effective way of repairing those neural pathways.

Depression medications, like SSRIs, have this same intent. SSRI stands for Selective Serotonin Reuptake Inhibitor and works by blocking the absorption of serotonin so that more of the neurotransmitter is available for your brain to use for things like sleep regularity and mood stability.

Researchers believe that the treatment with the best results is a combination of cognitive behavioral therapy and medication. Therapy alone is aimed at making these changes, but the greatest change in brain structures comes from a combination of two treatments. Regardless of which approach you choose, modern depression treatments are backed by current research and new treatments are being discovered every year.

Choose you. Choose treatment.

PRESS ON.

Note from the editor: Most of the individuals who experience success in rising above depression do so utilizing multiple methods, but treatment *nearly always includes* some form of cognitive behavioral therapy or professional counseling. For a more thorough discussion of types of therapy, go to the appendix.

Individuals do not need to be clinically diagnosed with depression (or other mental disorders) to seek treatment or therapy for depression.

CHAPTER 3:

The Depression Deception

by Keri Montgomery

You move slowly while everyone around you seems to move fast, as if they don't see the dull nothingness festering inside your mind. They're happy, and they smile, and they laugh out loud in a way you remember doing once, in what seems like a long-forgotten life, before the somberness set in.

Logically, you tell yourself the weighted feelings you're experiencing are temporary, maybe even the result of hard times or sudden loss or health struggles. You weren't always like this. You remind yourself that these moments of sadness are nothing more than the "whatever" stage you're in. At first, you might even sound convincing, stating, "I'm not depressed. Depression is for other people. People with worse problems."

That's the first self-deception.

Then, when your mind and your emotions continue to numb and that same heavy feeling sinks low in your rib cage as if a stone is binding to your heart, you take more notice. Something's different. Something's wrong. But you can handle it, and you decide it's possible to carry that stone around for a little while. It'll dissolve on its own with time, and without any effort.

That's the second self-deception.

Now, you're in a haze. Getting through the day requires more energy than you possess. Simple tasks that once were part of your daily routine begin to fit into two categories: *What I can handle* and

What I can't. And you feel resentment toward the "can't" list.

Others begin to notice a charge in your appearance, commenting that you look "tired" and asking, "Are you okay?" At times, you lie because it's easy. You say you're simply exhausted and build up a facade of fake excuses—the job is a nightmare, or the dog kept you up at night, or the kids' after school activities are wearing you out. Normal stuff. No big deal. When in actuality, you feel all those things and so much more—exhausted, worn out, longing for a break from the nightmare—but you simply smile and say, "I'm fine," because it's easier that way.

That's the third self-deception.

Then detachment begins. You find yourself growing ambivalent to the things and tasks you once cared for until full indifference takes over. The workdays, family events, school activities, projects, and appointments all begin to happen on autopilot, with a functionality and obligation more than a desire to enjoy the tasks.

You wonder if this is what zombies feel like.

Somewhere in the process, the bad days outnumber the good, and you experience a rock-bottom moment to rival all your previous lows. There may be tears, or anger, or devastation, or simply a panic that the stone of heavy emotions you've been carrying in your rib cage is going to devour your insides and leave nothing but a hollow core. You wonder if you can survive at all.

In that moment, a glimmer of realization shatters through the layers of self-deception: You have *Depression*.

You feel broken. You feel alone. And yet, that word, *Depression*, gives a tangible label to the nothingness. Rationality dictates that there are others with the same struggle, that depression is common, and that it's real. You realize you are among millions of others all fighting the same battle. Being *alone* is the illusion. You take in a deep breath, and you wonder how depression feels for them.

> "It feels like you're on a dirt road, and there's no end in sight. There's nothing to look at except dirt everywhere. Totally barren and the sky is a dull, gray-yellow inversion color. You keep walking and walking because

24

there's nothing else you can do except keep plodding along the empty road." — Laurie Richards

You wonder again if you can survive.

"Depression is like trying to describe the color of the sky to a blind person. How could anyone who hasn't experienced it ever really understand? People go through hardships, a bad break-up, being laid off, the death of loved ones, and they feel depression, anxiety, fear… But it's temporary. Time heals all wounds, as they say. But true depression, time doesn't heal it. You either find a way to make yourself strong enough to battle it, or it takes you. There's no gray area here. Depression kills. Unless of course we find a way to keep it from killing us." — Brandon T. Orgill

In time, you begin learning about this weighted stone in your rib cage—your own and very personal version of Depression.

"So hot that I am literally melting. Might as well be in Death Valley." — Nathan Croft

You notice triggers, moments of ordinary occurrences that bring you figuratively and sometimes literally to your knees—a missed deadline at work, or a disagreement with a spouse, or a friend who doesn't understand why you keep canceling plans. Fear creeps in. A fear that others will not understand your depression, even say "snap out of it," because they believe what you're feeling isn't real. Additional layers coat your stone of heavy emotions in your rib cage, adding to the weight—doubt, insecurity, worry, anxiety, and despair. You carefully control your interactions with others, deciding how much of your depression to reveal and how much to keep guarded.

At times you look in the mirror and wonder who—or what—you have become.

The Mirrored Face Feigned

I face the mirror facing me
And feign that I am all I see.
But deep behind that image hides the visage of my travesty.

Reflected features can't disguise

That other face whom I despise.
I shrink before the speculum's depiction of depravity,

a wretched wringing of the nerves,
a groping at internal curves,
that reaches through the glass to drive us both from
realms of sanity

to hateful acts of turpitude,
facsimiles of pulchritude,
which vivisect our reasonings and semblance of humanity

reduced to fragments vaporish,
that rave their gibbered gibberish
as we two wallow aimlessly through bouts of heart-bled blisterings,

a prelude to preoccupy
with dreams of ochre octopi
whose writhing clutches strangle thought amid duplicit whisperings

of harbors of fertility,
lain twisted in nihility,
enshrined beneath the tranquil deep of envied extirpations

'til shreds of echoed empathies
break through intrinsic apathies
to implement necessitated empty automations.

Escaped from mirrored scrutiny,
which spurs instinctive mutiny,
I leave behind the looking glass that hides the face of misery

Until tomorrow's ponderings
will lead cerebral wanderings
to turn another page within my repetitious history.
-- Jeremy Gohier

In your frustration, you question how depression, a thing you long
ago assumed was only about *sadness*, could give you such a variety
of negative emotions while leaving you feeling hollow at the same
time.

"Depression makes everything seem bigger and worse than it is. Life
becomes unbearably overwhelming. It also sucks the joy out of things that
make 'normal' people happy . . . and then it makes you feel guilty. Guilty

26

for not doing more, for not being more engaged, for not enjoying the things you know you should be grateful for. It makes you snappy because everything is an accusation, a confirmation of the voice in your head saying, 'You. Are. Failing.' It makes you angry that you can't seem to be better or give more than you're already giving, but it's almost impossible to give as much as you do." – Sabrina J. Watts

You find that sometimes friends and loved ones understand your depression, and sometimes they don't. That's simply a reality.

"I have been battling depression for more than thirty years after suffering a traumatic brain injury . . . Depression is a devastating feeling that there is no comfort nor hope. People have told me to go exercise, go to a movie, or call a friend. Oh, I wish it were that easy. I am told that everyone gets depressed. Yes, but not everyone battles depression on a daily basis. I am one of those... Depression is not just feeling blue or down. Depression is hell." – LeAnn Emery

And sometimes you must reach hell before you ask for help.

Recognizing You Need Help

by Camille Ballou

"My name is John, and I'm an alcoholic."

Those familiar words have been portrayed in some form or another since in 1935, when two recovering alcoholics, founders of Alcoholics Anonymous Bill Wilson and Dr. Bob Smith, created the famous 12-Step Addiction Recovery model. In meetings, addicts and recovering addicts are encouraged to state their name and admit publicly why they are there.

Why is this? Because admitting one has a problem is the first step. Admittance shows ownership; it feels vulnerable at first, but it is powerful. According to Wilson and Smith, before recovery could begin, they had to admit that they "were licked."

Let's translate this basic first step to depression. When and how do you recognize that you need help? At what point do you finally admit that you "are licked" by a force beyond your control?

27

Before admitting they have a problem and seeking help, many people with depression will spend some amount of time in denial. This stage is the gateway to the crucial step of admission and healing. There are two types of denial people experience when dealing with depression. The first is being partially or totally unaware. The second is seeing, understanding, and knowing that you have a problem and willfully denying it.

Unaware Denial

This type of denial is most common for those experiencing depression for the first time.

Julianne Kelsch, when describing her postpartum depression, said, "I hadn't considered that the constant pain in my gut and my inability to eat were a result of depression. It never crossed my mind that it wasn't normal to want to cry all the time, to survive every day and look forward to the short hours of oblivion at night before it all started over again. It never occurred to me that my existence had dramatically shifted from what it once was." This is a classic example of being unaware of how depression manifests.

So how do you recognize the shift that depression causes in your life as something more than feeling down? This can be exceptionally tricky, since it tends to happen gradually over time, much like the analogy of the boiling frog. A frog thrown into boiling water would likely hop out, but if the water is cool, the frog would stay and accidentally get himself boiled. Likewise, if you were to wake up one morning and experience your life instantly in a depressive state, you would be distraught enough to seek help. But given weeks, months, or even years to adapt to the changes that depression leaches into your life, you, not unlike the frog, may boil yourself a bit before realizing help is needed.

The good news is that like many of the diseases and ailments we may search the Internet about, depression has its own list of physical and emotional symptoms that can serve as warning signs. Physical symptoms can include changes in sleep habits, sex drive, weight gain or loss, fatigue, increase in chronic pain or new ailments (including, but not limited to, headaches, backaches, chest, or digestive issues). Emotional symptoms can include sadness, hopelessness, helplessness, numbness, loss if interest in previously enjoyable activities, irritability, anxiety, guilt, worthlessness, and thoughts of death or suicide.

Once side effects are recognized, it may still be difficult to recognize when to seek help.

When does it go from a temporary setback or case of the blues to something that requires intervention and professional help? This can be difficult to discern, considering everyone's experiences with mental health are different and equally valid. But generally speaking, when it impacts your ability to function normally at work and at home, intervention is needed. When your life is disrupted by depression in some regard. When life has taken on a facade that is not reflective of who you want to be. When you start self-medicating in other ways with food, alcohol, drugs, or sex, or even masking these dangerous coping mechanisms with seemingly healthy alternatives, like excessive exercise. When other people are noticing and are worried.

When willpower is not enough.

WILLFUL DENIAL

Some might ask why a depressed person who understands and knows they have a problem would not seek help.

> "Most depressives don't seek out help because a) they don't think it will work, b) they don't think they deserve it, and c) they don't have the energy.

> Most sufferers want to understand what's happening to them. They may research heavily, reading a lot of articles and forums, joining online support groups, and watching talks on depression. They will find some comfort in the fact that they're not alone, though it won't touch the actual depression itself. They'll gain some academic knowledge about what depression is and how to treat it, and they may decide to try some of the suggestions because what have they got to lose. More likely, though, they won't believe that any of these ideas could ever work for them, so they'll internalize them as

information but not act on them yet." – Heidi Robbins Tighe

Or perhaps they don't seek help because of the social stigma of having mental illness or an emotional disorder. Perhaps it is due to financial constraints. Perhaps, for those who have suffered with it long enough, it has become a part of them, and the idea of seeking help means making a change they are unwilling to make. Letting go of depression might scare them more than the depression itself. Usually, however, it is none of these.

Sufferer Dyany Munson recognizes that, "One of the crazy things about depression is how much it lies to you to get you to think you can't be helped. I can't think of another illness that does this, but know that most people with depression firmly believe that they can't be helped."

THE PARADIGM SHIFT

So how do you make the paradigm shift from denial to willing desire to change? Once depression has reached the point that professional help is needed, relationships with others have likely been affected. In casual relationships, people will remain oblivious to the depression, as the depressed person usually goes to great lengths to keep it that way. In speaking about her post-partum depression, Kelsch made the following observations:

> "I recognized during this time that I was ill and needed help and support. This was a difficult blow.
>
> I'd always been independent, and now I felt like a five year old child that needed to be spoon fed life again. It wasn't long before I realized that very few people around me recognized my illness. Most just knew something was wrong. The demands of life still pulled at me, the house still screamed at me, children still cried, my husband still expected a clean home, friends expected relationships, but I had nothing to offer any of them." – Julianne Kelsch

For more intimate relationships, it is likely that the friends or family will attempt to force the depressed individual to seek help. Sometimes this will be triggered by a major crisis or event—an emotional breakdown, discovery of self-harm, discovery of the depressed individual's distorted thinking, or other wherein someone on either side reaches their breaking point.

Whether casual or intimate, this is a delicate time, for the relationships may change based on how the friends or family members choose to respond to the depressed individual. Casual friends may reveal their own struggles or tell the depressed individual to "think positive" and suggest herbal supplements. Intimate friends and family will likely demand the depressed individual seek professional help if they have an informed enough perspective on the situation. If not, and this is their first encounter with mental illness and they lack a fundamental understanding, they may oppose professional help and insist the depressed person merely "snap out of it" somehow.

Dealing with relationships affected by depression can become as difficult as, and an unwelcome distraction to, dealing with the depression itself. And despite the insistence of others, true healing and change cannot occur until the depressed individual chooses to not only seek help but willingly take the steps necessary to heal. No amount of pressure from external relationships can enact the changes needed. While saving those relationships may be a vital component for seeking help and starting on the path of recovery, that motivation is not what ultimately heals. It culminates in a choice.

The Choice

by Keri Montgomery

Somewhere along your journey, you make a decision—battling to stay afloat doesn't have to be done alone, and that stone of heavy emotions in your rib cage doesn't need to weigh you down any longer. You choose to survive.

"I had slipped into a dark world—a place I'd previously glimpsed but never truly experienced. Like many before me, I didn't realize I'd entered this place until I was far too enveloped in it to change my course; the darkness swallowed me whole and I remained its prisoner far longer than I wanted to. But what I discovered in this darkness changed my entire life. I discovered that I was the only person who held the key to my deliverance. The day I chose my life over the darkness was the day my freedom began creeping back to me."   -- Julianne Kelsch

You make the choice in a single moment, and again in a hundred moments each day. But when the choice is made, you change your future from a picture to progress.

"Depression is like trying to save yourself from drowning with only a picture of a life vest. The saving grace comes from within and the strength of others." -- Christine Cottle

You put your trust in someone who cares, a person who is ready and willing to lend their strength to your battle, and you choose hope in spite of your depression.

Then you move forward one step at a time and keep breathing. You PRESS ON.

PRESS ON.

PART II

ENCOURAGEMENT AND TIPS TO PRESS ON

The next eighteen chapters contain more than 340 suggestions and tips for pressing on through depression. We recommend you peruse the chapters, listen to yourself, and choose just three to start.

Let the Rise begin.

CHAPTER 4:

The Goal is Happiness
of

The happy, white-picket fence dream of the past has become mired in mud and covered in algae. Views of what happiness is have morphed into unrealistic obsessions that make us less happy and more unfulfilled.

Today the desire for happiness resembles a life of luxury, ease, comfort, (instant) pleasure, and a clear life path. Not only do we believe happiness looks like vacation, we think it is an all-expense paid vacation that someone else plans, and includes a 100% satisfaction guarantee replacement trip in the event of storm, traffic delay, or temperatures outside of the preferred 65-80 degrees standard.

Have we come so far as an industrialized society that we have forgotten that discomfort, work, sadness, loss, and the occasional sore throat are all part of the journey?

Want to achieve happiness? Then stop obsessing over it.

Alan Wallace, one of the Western world's top experts in the practice of relaxed concentration, said, "Happiness is the default state of mind."

His statement implies that happiness is not something that you pursue, it is something you allow. Happiness is just being.

"Research has proven that external circumstances have a much smaller impact than we may think in determining our happiness.

Instead it appears that each of us is born with a happiness 'set point'. We are each predisposed to feel a certain level of happiness, and no matter the circumstances of our lives, we return to our set point," says Ezra Bayda in his book *Beyond Happiness*.

Perhaps a better goal is to be *in* each moment—fully present—to live and appreciate emotions and circumstances for what they are, even in temporary discomfort.

Finding joy in the experience of imperfection is a surer way to happiness than the pursuit of happiness as a goal.

So maybe happiness is within reach, and we just don't recognize it because it doesn't match the picture in our heads. We need to adjust expectations and align our expectations with our set points.

How do we adjust our expectations? That process is a mental one. Most of this chapter is a discussion of mental processes; an analysis of thinking:

- Thinking about thinking
- Reframing our thinking
- Changing our thinking processes
- Habitizing positive thinking

THE PSYCHOLOGY OF POSITIVITY

Ready to be in the moment? If I gave you a castle created from 5,051 Lego blocks, could you take the same small pieces and build them into something else—a racecar, a cat, or treasure chest? With instructions and time, indeed any number of creations would be possible. And if you engaged yourself in the building process, you'd be truly living in the moment.

Each of us possesses these building blocks in our brains. How they are constructed, based on the choices we make and the pathways used, determines a person's responses and personalizes their mind according to their experiences.

Neurons are the Legos of the central nervous system, including the brain. Neuroplasticity is the brain's capacity to change and adapt, or in other words, rearrange the blocks.

"The connections among the cells in our brains reorganize in response to our changing needs. This dynamic process allows us to learn from and adapt to different experiences.

Even when a nerve cell, or neuron, is damaged, 're-wiring' of the brain can make it possible for a function previously managed by a damaged area to be taken over by another undamaged area. The connections among the cells are infinitely receptive to this type of change and expansion."[v]

What does all that mean? Using techniques to engage your neurons, you can build and rewire your brain to improve your thinking processes. Does thinking solve everything? No, but intentional thinking is a critical part of treatment.

INTENTIONAL PROGRAMING

The concept of Intentional Programming was created by Charles Simonyi in reference to the field of computer programming, in which software source code was created that contains the precise intention programmers (or users) had in mind when they conceived their work.

The idea is simple enough: code the software so it will do exactly what you want it to do.

When we take our own brain building blocks and "code" them, we can actually rewrite our internal software and program our minds for the results we want to achieve.

We can program our brains using several methods presented in this book, from exercising to eating the right foods, but to build a new, depression-free design for our lives, we need to start with rewiring our brains.

The following section includes both broad-scale concepts and specific steps to implement the concepts. The selected are a few of the methods for programming happiness into our lives.

METACOGNITION: CHANGE YOUR THOUGHTS

Research proves (over and over again) that positive thinking powers mental and physical changes in the body. The brain's programming has the power to influence physical body outcomes and can outweigh even some medical diagnoses. Of course, it is easy to believe, but hard to implement, until you have formed a habit. Once habituated, the brain can take some of the pressure off going through the mental checklist to make it happen.

While positive thinking alone cannot be considered a cure for depression, science has shown that we do and become what we think about. Negative thoughts trigger downward spirals that lead into depression, where feelings of helplessness give way to hopelessness.

The brain takes thoughts, both positive and negative, and tries to enact them, to make them happen. Dr. Paul Jenkins says the first step to creating positive thoughts is simple (he also points out that simple and easy are not always the same thing):

Think about thinking.

"When you think about your thinking, it creates a space. In this space, choice exists. Until you see it as a choice, it is not. Choice is at the core of what we can do to improve our mental health.

When we are in a place of suffering, we don't see it as a choice. We think, 'I wouldn't choose this,' but until you see it as a choice, it is not."
-- Dr. Paul Jenkins

What is the resistance to metacognition and thinking about our thinking, as Dr. Jenkins suggests? The very idea that our thoughts are choices will send some people turning the other way, or passionately standing their ground, insistent they are not choosing depression or unhappy thoughts.

Dr. Jenkins responds to that scenario.

"Notice your defensive or resistant feelings, and then consider this: If you knew something you were doing might be contributing to your experience, then you would be in a position of choice. That is the key. We can empower people to get out of that mindset and say, 'What part is mine? What part am I doing that might be contributing to my experience?'"

For those still fuming at the suggestion that we are fueling our own depression, consider the following personal examples from Dr. Jenkins.

"My business partner and I flew from Salt Lake City into Las Vegas and then we rented a car and drove to Lake Havasu, Arizona, to teach a training class to police officers. After the training we used the drive back to Las Vegas to discuss the class and make plans for future trainings.

The dialogue was zealous, but not heated; we had many ideas and possibilities to voice. We continued on our way until a blaring sign stared us in the face: Welcome to California.

Somehow, we got so involved in our conversation, we missed the exit and drove out of Arizona, through Nevada, and into San Bernardino County, California.

I didn't consciously choose to miss the exit and drive in the wrong direction, but I looked down and saw my hands were indeed on the wheel. That is the part that bites, that is the part that stings."

Dr. Jenkins explains that it can be difficult to look at where you are and recognize you are there because *you drove there*. But that same fact should give us hope, because our hands are still on the wheel.

"One of my patients came to me struggling with severe clinical depression and suicidal thoughts. He probably wanted me to say that suicide isn't an option. But it is. And I told him so.

'So you are considering taking your own life. I want you to know that that is an option. One option. An alternative. A decision. You can do that. But it is a permanent, poor solution to a temporary, fairly easily resolved problem.'

The patient realized what I was getting at.

He responded with, 'I guess I just really need to change how I think.'

'Or not,' I said.

'But I want to,' he insisted.

'Ahh, that is different—when you want to change how you think. You

39

don't have to, you can continue thinking in a way that continues to make you miserable. Choice is the key.'"

Still mad at his insinuation that we are choosing some of the negative thoughts that fuel depression? Dr. Jenkins says we need to understand there are things we control and other things we don't. We don't control genetics and all of the body's chemical changes, but we need to be clear about what we can do.

> "Everyone is different, and every experience is different. That's just the way it is, so throw that whine out the window and either come up with a more valid complaint or deal with it. Sometimes our choices are limited, but we do have choices. I can choose how I am going to react. I can choose if I am going to see what I can learn from a situation. I can see if I will roll over and play dead, or get angry that life isn't fair. Of course it isn't 'fair' because there IS no 'fair.'" — Dyany Munson

Sometimes we are not looking for our choices. We are looking for justification. Dr. Jenkins says it is as though we are saying, "I deserve my misery; you are not going to take it away from me."

Treating people as if they are fragile doesn't help them. People are at risk to do things, like suicide. In fact, one year, *I knew a series of individuals who succeeded at suicide.* Nine people in my life. I lost nine people in a single year. Suicide is tragic.

But I still don't soft pedal with suicidal people. What most people need [when they are depressed or suicidal] is an affirming, confident approach, with PRINCIPLES that will solve, address, or resolve pain. Sometimes they just need someone to illuminate the obvious. We lose track of things because our consciousness doesn't always track that it is a choice. Our subconscious is running haywire telling us we can't handle it.

Dr. Susan Jeffers wrote a book titled, *Feel the Fear and Do It Anyway.* The title contains the most critical message of the whole book: we will have fears, but we need to act to help ourselves anyway.

At the root of every fear is the same belief: "I can't handle it." I am convinced that is ALWAYS a deception.

"People HANDLE things that are unthinkable. Elizabeth Smart, Bre Lasley, and others handled unthinkable abuse and violence. One of my clients, a ten-year-old child, found his parents murdered. I asked him if a year earlier he would have thought he could handle it if his parents were murdered. 'No way,' he replied. Then he paused and said, 'But you know what, I am handling it, huh'. Indeed, he was handling it." – Dr. Paul Jenkins

"Pain is inevitable, but misery is optional."

Tim Hansel stated it well. And long-time fibromyalgia and depression sufferer, Amy Furr agrees. She believes we must use our thoughts to control our reactions to difficult situations. "I have to live with these illnesses—*and everything that comes with them*—for the rest of my life. That's a fact of my life beyond my control. What I *can* control is my reaction to them; whether I choose to allow them to impair my life, or view them as blessings for my own life, as well as the lives of others, is up to me."

Use the power of creation, imagination, and positive thinking to make life better. How do we start the process to think about our thinking? Dr. Jenkins walks us through a simple scenario to help us awaken our minds to the possibilities.

PATHOLOGICAL POSITIVITY
Excerpts from *Pathological Positivity* by Dr. Paul Jenkins

"Do you notice the feeling of the shirt you have on?

You feel it all the time you wear it, but you don't notice the sensation unless you are reminded of it. If English is your primary language, it probably didn't occur to you that you are reading this...in English. Now that I bring it to your attention, you see it as an obvious fact. You didn't notice it, though, until I brought it to your attention—illuminating the obvious.

"As we come to understand how our mind processes our experience, we gain a higher level of control over how that happens. In this way, happiness is quite literally a choice. Between stimulus and response there is a space. In that space is our power to choose our response. In our response lies our growth and our freedom." — Viktor Frankl, *Man's Search for Meaning*

Between stimulus (the scene playing out) and response (from our initial emotional reaction to whatever we do about it), there is a space (before we feel or do anything). The space is often very small. Our responses, or reactions, can seem to be immediate.

In order to evaluate and judge [a situation or scenario] as good or bad, our mind imagines something better or worse than what It actually is.

Better and worse carry a judgment. With that judgment comes an emotional charge.

We can always imagine something better than "It". No matter how good our circumstance, something could always be better.

When we compare "It" with something worse, we feel better about "It".

From a psychological perspective, we have to evaluate "It.". As Dr. Frankl observes, evaluation happens constantly and automatically. Anything better or anything worse than "It" is all imagined. This gives us some control over how we feel in any situation because we get to choose which of these imagined scenarios we will use to evaluate "It."

We are powerful creators. Just as our minds constantly and continually evaluate "It," they also constantly look toward what is coming.

Our minds must imagine what is to be because it doesn't exist yet. The only place where what is to be can exist is in our imagination. This is a good thing. In fact, it's great because imagination is essential to creation.

The amazing sculptor Michelangelo said, "I saw the angel in the marble and carved until I set him free."

Follow Michelangelo's counsel and imagine [what is to be]. Imagination is what makes the doing part relatively simple.

When we imagine something better coming, we feel better. Imagining something better is just as legitimate as imagining something worse – but it feels good.

This is how we **choose** how we feel. Although we may not directly choose our feelings, we can choose which imagined scenario we use to anticipate and create "what is to be" that in turn creates the feelings we would like to have.

Most people would not intentionally go out and make life worse, but when we imagine it all the time, when we allow ourselves to have negative thoughts and worry, then that is exactly what is happening.

The only reality is where you are. The rest is imaginary.

So, what does it boil down to? When we imagine what is going to happen is worse than where we are, that is the very definition of anxiety." – Dr. Paul Jenkins

DOUSING DOUBT

For Blen Harline, negativity showed in his self-criticism and unhealthy comparisons. His habit made him question his own value. (Read his full essay in Part III.)

> "With depression, comparing myself to others is totally detrimental. I never cease to notice the strengths obvious in others that I don't have:
>
> 'Look how she talks to her friends, the ease at which she can make them laugh and follow her every word.'
>
> 'Look how people gravitate to that guy! Look at how handsome he is!'
>
> The thing is, the monster [depression] doesn't always know what actually matters to me. It's assuming that what's important to some people and what their talents are, is something I should be good at.
>
> *I have to remind myself to stop using someone else's tape measure to measure my own self-worth.*" – Blen Harline

Before we can use our own tape measures, we must first acknowledge we are using another form of measurement. Science has shown it is nigh impossible to just eliminate a bad habit, says Charles Duhigg, author of the bestselling book, *The Power of Habit.*

The key is to change a negative habit to a positive one, using some form of "trigger" to signal our brains we need to make a change.

"My 5-year-old is a worrier at bedtime. We have taught her that when you feed them, worries grow. When she worries we ask her if she is growing her worry tree or her gratitude tree, and then help her think of good things instead.

Our minds are funny things. If you simply try **not** to feel sad, or blue, or anxious, it's probably not going to work. Give your brain something to replace it. When a sad thought comes in, look around you and find something good to replace it. It can be as simple as "the sun is shining" or "those flowers are beautiful". – Celeste Noland

Use the following simple steps to begin the change process.

HOW TO ELIMINATE NEGATIVITY
AND REFRAME A THOUGHT INTO A POSITIVE

by Christy Monson, LSW, Family Therapist

1. **Notice the negative thought.** (Acknowledge the thought and that you are thinking it.)
2. **Stop it.** (Use any of the following as a signal to halt the negative thought process.)
   a. Visualize a STOP sign in your head.
   b. Wear a rubber band on your wrist and flip it every time there's a negative thought.
   c. Pinch yourself.
   d. Create a charity/money jar and deposit a quarter/dollar for every negative thought.
3. **Reframe your negative thought into a positive one.**
   a. Think of a potentially positive outcome out of a negative situation. (I missed the train, but I could meet someone new on the bus.)
   b. Be grateful something worse didn't happen.
   c. Imagine a stronger future.
   d. Decide what you can learn from your situation.
4. **Dwell on the positive thought.**
   a. Keep a positive thought journal.
   b. Think about the next logical step to the positive thought.

Notice. Stop. Reframe. Dwell.

Let's get down to specifics. Eliminate the negatives.

- **All or nothing thinking is always negative.** Whenever a sentence contains "always" or "never," kick it out of your head. Things are never black and white. If I asked fifty people to solve a problem, I'd probably get at least forty-six different answers. Eliminate phrases like, "It's always my fault. It's my fault you lost your job." (Notice the "always.") Other people are responsible for their own choices. Not you.
- **Imagining the worst.** "Something bad will happen." Things are only "bad" or "good" by the value we put on them. Find something good about your situation. Sometimes we look for disasters. This is disaster-thinking. A friend said the other day, "You can't leave me in this car when it's idling. It may blow up." Even in jest, when we allow our thoughts to run wild we are telling others, and ourselves, that the worst will come.
- **Self-doubt.** "Anyone can do my job." Doubting yourself has the same effect as imagining the worst. Stop thoughts of self-doubt. Keep a positive attitude about yourself. Find your good. Identify things you do or ways you do things that are unique, beneficial, or helpful.

We all can learn from our mistakes. In fact, we gain more from our losses than we do from our victories because we are learning and growing. Look at a situation that didn't result as you wanted it to and *challenge your assumption*. Find something good about it.

Thinking is a habit. Make it a positive one.

THE FLIP SIDE
by Jodi Orgill Brown

Sometimes the most important thing we can do is take the painting off the wall and turn it upside down. Only after we change our perspective can we see it is still beautiful artwork!

Indeed, there is a flip side to every situation. Before my brain tumor, I didn't have a clue about the depression beast that terrorizes so many people I love. But when the doctors excavated the mass from my brain, it seemed a part of my life was carved away, too.

I didn't know that "saving my life" would mean giving up one life in exchange for another. The type A, "get-'er-done girl" in me is still there, but she is buried under a mess of migraines, dizzy spells, facial paralysis, and nerve pain. I've struggled with the new, slow, sometimes tripping pace in my second life.

For years I fought between taking care of myself and taking care of my family. To get the sleep my brain needs, I went to bed earlier and got up later than most of my household, including my young children. Guilt racked me, knowing that while I slept, my elementary school kids had to get themselves up, dressed, fed, lunches packed, and out the door. The other mothers, I presumed, sang through the morning rituals and then kissed the heads of their little ones as they dropped them off at school, all while I stayed in bed.

Then one day it hit me. How could I possibly raise responsible children without giving them responsibilities? How could they become self-reliant without having to be self-reliant? It wasn't until I turned the frame on my own way of thinking that I saw all the good that came from our situation. My children are well on their way to becoming independent, functioning, aware, caring, contributing members of society—it just came in a different way than I expected. Turns out, some of our worst challenges are also our greatest opportunities, but only when we choose to see them that way.

Life is neither for you nor against you. But if you believe the rain falls only on your head, you may drown instead of getting watered.

To be alive is to have experiences;
to live life is to learn from experiences.

ASSIGNING LABELS

International bestselling author Angie Fenimore struggled with deep depression for years before the suicide attempt and near-death experience that pushed her to record the account in *Beyond the Darkness*. She still struggles with depression, more than twenty-five years later. But now she has tools to deal with the darkness.

Angie focuses on separating circumstances and thoughts from the labels we attach to them.

> "Circumstances are just circumstances. That is all they are.
>
> We assign circumstances with labels, good and bad. Circumstances are the backdrop of real life, but we collapse our relationships with the circumstances exist. *We stage.*
>
> We assign a label to a situation, and *then* it takes on meaning."
> – Angie Fenimore

Circumstance: An empty bank account   *Label*: Bad

Circumstance: Lots of money   *Label*: Good

But what if the empty bank account is simply because you changed banks? Is it still bad? Or what if a load of money is the result of robbing a bank? Is it still good?

The truth is, circumstances are different from the labels we assign to give them meaning. When we keep circumstances and thoughts separated from labels, we can process them without suffering *because* of them.

Angie related the following true story to illustrate her point. We would say a broken-down car is bad. When my car broke down, we were in a bind. My kids go to school twenty-five miles from our home, so we had to figure out a way to get them to school. We spent hours and sorted out the schedules for public transportation. The kids got proficient at getting themselves back and forth to school. And they experienced themselves in powerful and self-reliant roles. I wanted to make it very clear that they can have anything they want in this life—even with a broken down car. We'd assign the circumstance *now* as a good thing.

But that is not the end of the story. I spent hours of time walking back and forth to bus stops and train stations, so much so that I lost weight. And on the train, I had time to write. So, even though one 45-minute appointment took me eight hours, that time was useful and amazing. And the connections I made have been quite profound.

One thing I learned from my near-death experience is the only thing we take with us is the relationships we have. And those relationships are with everyone around us: the train engineer, bus driver, cashier, and teacher, and not just our family and friends.

The point is, the circumstances are just the circumstances. That is all they are. And we get to choose. We get to choose what thoughts we hold on to, what meaning we give them, and what kind of relationships we are going to have.

What You Believe is True

Your beliefs actually run the show. What you believe is broadcast in all you do. You become a magnet for these beliefs. It is the very reason why even subtle messages, on t-shirts, in music, on tattoos, will attract certain experiences and people to you. The messages you engage with resonate with you. If you have a relationship with those thoughts, like you generated them, it creates an emotional charge, and that is where the trouble begins. You will take ownership of the ideas and thoughts, as if they were your creation.

For example, the thought "I'm fat" is meaningless unless we are triggered emotionally by it. Which is where "belief" can empower or destroy. If I believe that I'm fat, no big deal, unless I *also* believe that being fat makes me unworthy of love, repulsive, and makes my husband less than faithful to me, *and* I also have an emotional experience of being unworthy of love. I could even believe I'm fat and unlovable and it would not impact me unless I also had the emotional kick. It's the emotional charge, paired with the belief, that is the culprit.

As we become possessive of thoughts, we not only believe them, we subconsciously seek to prove them. This can be especially dangerous given that some of our thoughts can be inherited in our DNA, psyche, and in inherited attitudes and thoughts from family. Though we may have pre-dispositions passed to us, it does not mean you are destined to those.

The darkness or light within you will come out. You become a magnet for that kind of thought. — Angie Fenimore

So how do we process dark thoughts that come to us, in order not to take ownership of them or assign labels to them? The following are the steps Fenimore recommends to elevate yourself above the thoughts:

1. **Control the environment you are in.** Be conscious about where you are, the messages around you, what you read and listen to, and even the messages you are wearing.

2. **Acknowledge dark thoughts, but do not engage with them.** Allow yourself a moment of, "Oh, that was an interesting thought!", but **do not wrap emotion around dark thoughts**. Do not relate to them. Do not believe them. Do not allow an emotional charge to pair with a thought or belief.

3. **Let go of fear.** Fear is one of the highest levels of darkness with which you can resonate. When you engage fear, it amplifies whatever else you are dealing with. Release fear by erasing the stories in your mind. Fear projects forward, but future events haven't happened, they are all imaginary. So erase them. (Picture yourself with an eraser, blotting out all the what ifs, failures, and sad endings.)

4. **Let it go.** Let go of the dark thought after you acknowledge it. You already encountered the thought, but you do not have to answer it. Dismiss it before you ruminate on it or let it take seed within you.

5. **Let light in.** When you allow dark thoughts to pass through you, you create space for light to come in. Thought space in our brains is a vacuum; you must fill the empty space, so choose things that will elevate you and empower you. It's impossible to not think any thoughts, so sing, recall a favorite memory, or practice a poem, but have a positive go-to thought ready to fill the void.

As you practice the steps of disconnecting thoughts and circumstances from labels and meanings, you will be emboldened with power and lifted by light.

SELF-TALK

by Jessica Thornton

We all hold internal conversations as we go through our days, and sometimes our nights. Psychologists have identified one important type of these inner monologues as "self-talk," in which you provide opinions and evaluations on what you're doing as you're doing it. You can think of self-talk as the inner voice equivalent of sports announcers commenting on a player's successes or failures on the playing field.

Unlike that sports commentary, which athletes never hear while they're competing, you can actually "hear" what your own self-talk is saying. When this is upbeat and self-validating, the results can boost your <u>productivity</u>. However, when the voice is critical and harsh, the effect can be emotionally crippling.

Consider what happens after you've done something embarrassing. Does your inner voice say, "That was sure stupid"? How about if you haven't even done anything wrong or stupid at all, but your self-talk is just as critical? This **destructive** type of self-talk causes you to question yourself so constantly that you can soon become paralyzed with doubt and uncertainty.

As an example of how this destructive self-talk works, consider the following scenario. You're at a small party hosted by one of your family members when the conversation turns into a debate about the latest episode of a popular TV show. You express an opinion that the others disagree with, and although there are no facts involved, you feel that you've just made a huge *faux pas*. You hated the episode, and everyone else thought it was among the best of all time. The self-talk chatter starts to build in your head: "You should've kept your mouth shut. Why can't you just keep quiet when you disagree with someone? You came across as completely ignorant. They looked at you like you were nuts." The more you listen to your own self-criticism, the more you retreat from the actual conversation going on around you. Within a few minutes, you feel so horrible that you just leave the party, running through the whole episode in your mind over and over until you wish you had never even gone in the first place.

Turn the situation around and imagine the scene but instead, you respond with **constructive self-talk.** Nothing has changed— you've still expressed views that differed from everyone else's. You thought it was the worst episode of all time, and they thought it was the best. Your self-talk, though, takes the following form: "I'm glad I stuck to my guns." "I think I expressed myself very clearly."

"It's just a TV show; so what if I didn't like it!" In constructive self-talk, you cheer yourself on, focus on the positive aspects of a situation, and allow yourself to feel good about what you've done.

Positive Self-talk is a habit you can develop using methods similar to changing from negative thought patterns to positive ones.

AFFIRMATIONS

You really are what you think, which means we need to choose carefully the thoughts we have about ourselves. The word affirmation comes from the Latin *affirmare*, originally meaning, "to make steady, strengthen."

> "Affirmations are proven methods of self-improvement because of their ability to rewire our brains. In the sequence of thought-speech-action, affirmations play an integral role by breaking patterns of negative thoughts, negative speech, and, in turn, negative actions."
>
> Affirmations are basically a form of auto-suggestion, and when practiced deliberately and repeatedly, they reinforce chemical pathways in the brain, strengthening neural connections (think Lego bricks).
>
> Evidence suggests that the repetitive use of positive affirmations can successfully treat conditions of low self-esteem, depression, and other mental health issues.
>
> Though some people can use affirmations to overcome depression and negative thinking, the tactic is not a one-size-fits-all solution. Some people may view affirmations as "wishful thinking," and of course, mindset is critical in experiencing success, with affirmations, as well as with other forms of self-talk and positivity. You must believe, even just a little, that your efforts will pay off. Those who don't believe will rarely give these techniques a try.
>
> Try looking at positive affirmations this way: many of us do repetitive exercises to improve our body's physical health and condition. Affirmations are like exercises for our mind and outlook; these positive mental repetitions can reprogram our thinking patterns so that, over time, we begin to think, and act, in a new way. I love to write affirmations on my bathroom mirror and hang positive quotes in my closet (someplace I see it regularly).

Instead of what I might hear myself saying, (negative self-talk), I repeat the affirmations as much as I can until they become automatic thoughts.

I'm afraid. **I am safe.**

My life means nothing. **My life is meaningful.**

No, I can't. **Yes, I can!**

I hate myself. **I am beautiful and strong!**" – Jeni Farner

Not sure how to create your own affirmation? Start with "I am," "I feel," "My," and "I have" statements that reflect the kind of person you want to be or goals you've set for yourself. Affirmations are powerful for every area of your life, including relationships and love, professional success, happiness, confidence, health and wellbeing, spirituality and peace.

- I am the architect, designer, and builder of my life. I can achieve what I dream.
- I power my life with actions of intention and outward thinking.
- My life is a gift. I do not waste time on trivialities, I invest time in people.
- My relationships are meaningful and I can enhance them every day through selfless service to those I love.
- I forgive easily and ask for forgiveness often to stay in check with others and to lift unnecessary burdens from my soul and spirit.
- I share wisdom that helps my family and strengthens faith in God.
- My fears are in the past. I have the strength and courage to move forward.
- I exude happiness and I find joy in the simple things.
- My immune system is strong and fights all foreign cells and illnesses.
- I see into souls and look for the strength within others.
- My abilities are limitless. I can achieve my goals and conquer my challenges.
- I am dynamic, intelligent, and powerfully influential.

Not quite right? Try the affirmation used in the 1993 classic movie,

Cool Runnings. Look in the mirror for this one.

"I see pride! I see power! I see a bad-ass mother who don't take no crap off of nobody!"

No matter which affirmations you choose, make a commitment to yourself to say them every day to give your mind the chance to enact these mind-building phrases. And remember, when in doubt or need, you can always call upon the strength of the affirmation in *Invictus* to power yourself to a better life today.

"I am the master of my fate; I am the captain of my soul."
-- William Ernest Henley, *Invictus*

POWER YOUR SMILE

What is the reason that "fake it until you make it" actually works? Because "faking it" is often pretending we are happy (even if we are suffering inside) and that includes smiling, even when we don't feel like it. But smiling produces immediate results. If you have ever doubted the power of a smile, just grin and see what happens next.

In his article "Smile: A Powerful Tool," Alex Korb Ph.D. shares, "Scientists have known for a long time that emotions are accompanied by numerous changes in the body, from elevation in the heart rate to flexion of the zygomatic major muscle (i.e. smiling). However, we've come to understand more recently that it's a two way street. Your brain actually pays attention to what your body is doing, and it affects your emotions. The good news is that while it's sometimes hard to control our emotions, it's much easier to control our muscles. So … smile. Your smile is a powerful tool."

Studies show the power of smiling is both immediate and contagious. Smiling stimulates the reward mechanisms in the brain, which release endorphins and create a natural high. And, better still, the action is naturally imitated by others, so everyone around you will also benefit from your smile, first because of their reaction to you, second because they will naturally copy your facial expression.

The effect of smiling is so intense that even the imitation of a smile can trigger the positive endorphin rush, and sometimes even decrease pain. In fact, a study by Dr. Paula Niedenthal showed the simple act of engaging the smile muscles, by holding a pencil or pen in your mouth, produces the same boosting results as the real thing.

"It is a simple thing, almost too easy to mention. But when I smile, I really do feel better. I can't be sad or depressed when I am smiling. That's all it is." – C.M. Danlon

Studies have also shown the effects of smiling are stronger when you smile for at least two minutes, and are greater still when you see your own smile. Therefore, perhaps the best way to start your day—or turn a down day up— is to stand in front of the mirror and smile. (Hold it, hold it, count down the two minutes before you stop.) This small action will initiate a powerful process in your brain and body that will make you happy, at least for a while.

If you don't feel like smiling, force a small grin, or pop that pencil between your lips and let the vibes flow.

PRESS ON.

Quick Positivity Can-Do Tips:

- Envision the good. Think of three good things that could happen today because of your actions.
- Name something you do well.
- Choose a difficult situation from your past and reframe it in a positive light to see how you, or someone else, is better because of your struggle.
- Write down three things that went well today and why they went well.
- Practice daily affirmations by voicing the actions, traits, characteristics, behaviors and outcomes you desire for yourself. Start simple: I am kind, honest, and thoughtful and I believe in myself. I make the best of situations and I enjoy helping others.
- Make a list of activities that you enjoy. Try to incorporate at least one favorite activity into your daily routine.
- Pick out beauty in three things or moments in your day. From noticing the flowers to receiving a compliment, find the beautiful amongst the normal or dreary.
- Savor a moment. Pick something small and just enjoy--a few extra minutes in the shower or the taste of your morning pick-me up drink are perfect ways to savor the start of the day.

CHAPTER 5:

High Hormones: How to Be Happy
Do

Tired of thinking about thinking? However useful it is to analyze and reprogram our thinking habits, mindful attention to thought is not enough.

Thinking is the basis for action, but it is not action itself. We can *over*think situations and drive ourselves crazy. To fully enjoy the benefits of changed perspectives or positive thinking, we must physically connect our bodies to our thoughts—through our actions. Without the physical enacting of our thoughts, we create disconnect between the physical self and mental self.

If depression and other mood disorders result from changes to normal chemical and hormonal production, release, and processing within the body, does it stand to believe that happiness is our body's default setting?

This chapter focuses on the basic science behind happiness, how what we think and do create physiological responses in our bodies.

According to a 2008 study published in Psychological Science, inherited genes seem to account for fifty percent of our happiness. But, whether your natural tendency is to be bright and cheery or solemn and sad, your choices can help you experience a brighter, happier life.

"Being in a positive state has significant impact on our motivation, productivity, and wellbeing. No sane person would be opposed to having higher levels in those areas." — Thai Nguyen, The Huffington Post

The control and moderation of mental wellbeing come from naturally-occurring hormones and neurotransmitters in the body. Activities and lifestyle factors either increase or decrease these hormones, which affect our feelings of happiness. We might not have a money tree, but we can have a happiness tree. Dopamine, serotonin, oxytocin, and endorphins are the quartet responsible for our happiness. Many events can trigger these neurotransmitters, but rather than being in the passenger seat, there are ways we can intentionally cause them to flow.

THE FINAL FOUR

ENDORPHINS

Endorphins are your body's natural painkillers. They act as pain blockers, building protective carriers that keep us from experiencing the negative effects of pain, which cause us to cease activity. Some endorphins function as neurotransmitters, but most act primarily by altering the effects of neurotransmitters by *limiting* or *prolonging* their effects, hence the pain-killer effect. Exercise releases endorphins. Though this originally helped man to fight through pain to escape predators, today we only produce endorphins when we perform anaerobic exercises, since endorphins help us to keep going even after we deplete our oxygen stores.

DOPAMINE

This neurotransmitter manages your brain's reward system and affects neurons involved in voluntary movement, learning, memory, emotion, and possibly in response to novelty. Praise and pleasure reward you with dopamine hits that increase feelings of wellbeing. Boost dopamine levels by setting realistic goals (washing the car every week or sticking to your workout schedule), and then achieving them. Setting goals and not achieving them increases negative feelings, including self-doubt and guilt, which can further sink you in the abyss of depression. Seek out pleasurable healthy endeavors, and the activities and dopamine boosts will have a positive impact on your life. But be careful, "pleasure, which is short-term, addictive, and selfish, works on dopamine,"[vi] so keep your choices and activities well balanced.

Serotonin

Serotonin is known as a bad-mood and depression buster. As Seth Godin says, "Happiness is long-term, additive and generous. It's giving, not taking. It works on serotonin." [vii]

It affects neurons involved in sleep, appetite, sensory perception, temperature regulation, pain suppression, and mood. Thai Nguyen, in the Huffington Post, explains, "Serotonin flows when you feel significant or important. Loneliness and depression appears when serotonin is absent. Unhealthy attention-seeking behavior can also be a cry for what serotonin brings."

Serotonin's fifteen-minutes of fame came as research showed the power of serotonin as an antidepressant. Nearly 80% of the antidepressants on the market are SSRIs, selective serotonin reuptake inhibitors, which increase serotonin levels at extracellular levels by inhibiting reabsorption into presynaptic cells so they are able to bind with postsynaptic cells and remain in the synapse longer. (Note: Low levels of the neurotransmitters serotonin and norepinephrine have been associated with severe depression.)

> "Reflecting on past significant achievements allows the brain to re-live the experience. Our brain has trouble telling the difference between what's real and imagined, so it produces serotonin in both cases. It's another reason why gratitude practices are popular. They remind us that we are valued and have much to value in life. If you need a serotonin boost during a stressful day, take a few moments to reflect on past achievements and victories." – Barry Jacobs, Princeton neuroscientist

Still the most effective and natural way to increase serotonin is through daily exercise. A walk does wonders for your body, mind, and your mood, so stop standing around and start walking somewhere.

Oxytocin

Both a neurotransmitter and a hormone, oxytocin is often called "the love hormone." Researchers from Claremont University in

California have linked the effect of oxytocin to higher life satisfaction levels in women. (It may play a greater role in women's physiology and happiness compared to men's.) Spending time with loved ones and being kind to others stimulates oxytocin. Stress blocks the release of oxytocin, so heed everyone's favorite advice from the doctor and "manage your stress" for best results.

PLAYER OR PUPPET

Before drowning yourself in hormones, heed some wise words on how industry can manipulate natural feelings, so you don't get taken for a ride.

From the "The Pleasure/Happiness Gap" by Seth Godin[viii]

"Pleasure (dopamine) and happiness (serotonin) feel like they are substitutes for each other, different ways of getting the same thing. But they're not. Instead, they are things that are possible to get confused about in the short run, but in the long run, they couldn't be more different.

Both are cultural constructs. Both respond not only to direct, physical inputs (chemicals, illness) but more and more, to cultural ones, to the noise of comparisons and narratives.

Marketers usually sell pleasure. That's a shortcut to easy, repeated revenue. Getting someone hooked on the hit that comes from caffeine, tobacco, video or sugar is a business model. Lately, social media is using dopamine hits around fear and anger and short-term connection to build a new sort of addiction.

On the other hand, happiness is something that's difficult to purchase. It requires more patience, more planning and more confidence. It's possible to find happiness in the unhurried child's view of the world, but we're more likely to find it with a mature, mindful series of choices, most of which have to do with seeking out connection and generosity and avoiding the short-term dopamine hits of marketed pleasure."

To find long-term *real* happiness, start moving, achieving, and loving.

PRESS ON.

Quick Happiness Can-Do Tips:

Ways to boost your body's natural painkilling ability with the following endorphin-increasing activities:

- Exercise. (Especially to cope with chronic pain.)
- Eat spicy food. (Your tongue has receptors that react to spice by sending messages to your brain that are similar to pain signals, causing your brain to trigger the release of endorphins.)
- Smell vanilla or lavender scents.
- Engage in loving sex with a committed partner.

Ways to increase your dopamine levels:

- Set daily, weekly or monthly goals. (The more attainable goals you set, the merrier, since they give you positives to strive towards, and thereby greater likelihood of getting the "high" of achievement.)
- Set exercise goals, since dopamine increases in tandem with serotonin and endorphins when you exercise.
- Eat protein-rich foods.
- Listen to music.

Ways to increase your serotonin levels:

- Spend time in the sun, since sunlight causes your body to produce Vitamin D, which triggers the release of serotonin.
- Think happy thoughts.
- Consume foods like milk and corn, since they contain tryptophan, a substance that your body converts to serotonin.
- Do a low-intensity workout; since your body produces serotonin when it is performing aerobic exercise, as opposed to the endorphins it produces during anaerobic exercise.
- For the best mood boost with the least negative effect, choose healthy, high-fiber sources of carbs such as dense whole-grain bread or quinoa.

Ways to increase your oxytocin levels:

- Get a massage. Relaxing your muscles in combination with physical contact trigger the release of oxytocin.
- Show love. Give a hug or put your arm around a loved one.
- Cuddle.

CHAPTER 6:
Triggers

If you don't pull the trigger, the gun won't fire. The science isn't as simple, but the result is. In the struggle with depression, we have to learn not to pull our own triggers.

> "Learn to identify the triggers that start your downward spirals and you'll have a powerful tool in rising above depression. Episodes of depression and anxiety typically begin with some kind of trigger. It may be a catastrophic or traumatic event or loss; it can be something simple, like a conversation that stirs up feelings of insecurity, something seen on TV or read; it can be caused by compromised health or pregnancy/hormone fluctuation. The elderly are prone to depression if they lose their sense of purpose, are isolated, and struggle with age related health issues. People with the genetic predisposition are more susceptible to triggers, but that doesn't necessarily guarantee a person will become depressed. There is a broad range of symptoms and severity. One person's form of depression may not be as challenging as another's." – Rebecca Clayson

Most of us have specific activities, thoughts, habits, or patterns that trigger anxiety, negativity, frustration, and depression. When we learn to pinpoint specific triggers, we can also learn to minimize the occurrences in our lives.

For Chelsea*, the biggest trigger for depression, and subsequently suicidal thoughts, was Friday nights. During the week, she put in forty hours at work and kept up on basic household responsibilities and personal tasks. But when Friday nights came around and she found herself home alone, perceiving that the rest of the world was out enjoying life, she crumbled. Her exhaustion set in, her thoughts turned negative, and her weekends spiraled into long bouts of sleeplessness, anxiety, and depression. She could barely function enough to survive, spending most of her time drinking or medicating herself away from overwhelming thoughts and feelings.

"What is wrong with me? I am broken. Something in me is broken, and I can't fix it. I've tried, I promise I've tried," she repeated time and time again, "but no matter what I do, nothing gets better," she lamented to a friend.

It was Chelsea's friend who noticed that the hopeless texts, crying emojis, and even goodbye messages came, with startling regularity, on Friday nights.

At a time when Chelsea seemed happy and positive, her friend broached the subject.

"I had never realized it before, but she was right. I fell into the exact same pattern every weekend without even knowing I was doing it. In some ways, I set myself up to fall," Chelsea said.

Her friend suggested Chelsea make plans for Friday nights, even if she didn't have a social engagement. Plans could include anything from grocery shopping to cleaning, to exercising, or even indulging in a little pampering time, anything that would give her activities or time in which positive thoughts could flow.

Long-time sufferer Erin Grimley stated that identifying her triggers was one of the first steps of empowerment, where she actually felt like she had some control over the depression that had controlled her for so long.

> "It was when I was in the hospital that I learned the importance of finding my triggers. I didn't want to be in the hospital, but I knew I needed help or I was going to give into the feelings of hopelessness I felt from depression. As part of my therapy, I was required to spend hours thinking about and recording my triggers. It was the first time I understood that the things I do can trigger my depression.

Years later, Erin is still working daily to manage both triggers and depression, but she knows the importance of keeping triggers at bay.

"I found that some relationships were triggers for me. Unhealthy relationships and toxic people ruled my life, and I let them because I got sucked into it. I learned I had to let go and not care so much about what people thought about me. They aren't right, anyway, so I know now that I can't let it get to me. I can't let their thoughts and words change and hurt me. It is still hard, but I am getting better at it." — Erin Grimley

Erin also found positive things to replace the triggers. "Exercise is important for me, too. I know that if I am not exercising, I am more prone to feeling down. Now I embrace myself and my body," Grimley says.

In delving into exercise, she found a passion in pole dancing, which requires enormous strength, coordination, rhythm, and timing.

"I have to focus and have positive energy in order to do a pole routine. I can't lose control of my thoughts or I fall. Turns out that mastering your thoughts is a big step to dealing with depression," Erin said.

Not a morning person? Neither is Landon. In fact, every time he had a job that required him to work mornings, anxiety took over his life and nearly always resulted in depression. The cycle repeated itself for years. The excitement and anticipation of the first few weeks on a new job masked the trigger, but the moment the routine set in, the negative cycle started.

"I worried about whether I would get enough sleep, whether my alarm would go off, whether I would feel well enough to work. Then I wouldn't be able to sleep, so I'd toss and turn all night worrying. By morning, I'd have to call in sick because I was a total mess from not sleeping the night before.

Ultimately, I took a cut in pay and started in a new industry so I could have a little more control over my work hours. I am willing to put in the time, but when I realized that morning work caused such a problem for the rest of my life, I knew I had to make a change. – Landon*

M.K. adds, "I've had to train myself to see the triggers that set off my anxiety before it turns into major depression. I had to teach myself how to get out of my comfort zone."

"The constant fast pace of the world today, including the flashing, buzzing, lights and sensory overload, can trigger anxiety, fear, sadness, overstimulation, and feelings of isolation. As a society, we have become accustomed to controlling our surroundings with a fingertip or simple voiced phrase. We sometimes forget that we do not hold all environmental controls. If you are not prepared, any number of scenarios can throw you into a storm. It wasn't until I was married with kids that I realized I had suffered from depression and anxiety all my life. From the time I was young, I struggled with feelings of being alone and unsupported. It's not that I didn't have parents around, but their time was all focused on my brother, who had cancer and eventually died.

By the time I checked into a hospital, I was suicidal and felt betrayed and mostly alone. I missed my son's birthday, I missed him cutting his pirate cake.

From the therapies I've learned that I have to speak up for myself. I cannot care so much or believe what people think or say." — Erin Grimley

Erin learned that she has many triggers, so she has to be mindful of the people and activities in her life. But she also knows how to manage her life to bypass her triggers. "I am really good at avoiding triggers. Point blank. I know what they are and now I'll do anything to avoid them."

She discussed examples of her triggers, as follows:

- "When I feel like I don't have control, or when people are trying to tell me what to do, I don't like that. Causes me anxiety."
- "Black Friday and I are not friends. Can't do it. Anything where I have to compete for things in a crowd, I won't go. I won't even take my kids to Easter egg hunts. I don't want to be in a position where some parent is telling their kid to knock my kid over. I don't like the chaos and competition to get a little prize."
- "I can't handle phone calls about overwhelming topics. I have to take things in smaller doses."
- "I've also learned *when* I need to stay busy. I prepare myself when I know something is coming. As the anniversary of my

friend's death approaches, I know I have to take extra care to do the right things and avoid certain situations, or they will trigger my depression."

As Erin mentioned, sometimes people can be triggers. Is there a certain someone who always brings out the worst in you? Many of us have friends we gossip with, complain to, or are negative around. Some friendships seem like more work than they are worth, or we leave feeling frustrated or down in the dumps.

Recognize the toxic relationships in your life and LEAVE THEM BEHIND. Let them go so you don't fall into the unhealthy cycles these individuals knowingly or unknowingly create.

When you find yourself around an individual who is always complaining, excuse yourself. Or, depending on the relationship, maybe confront the person. Sometime people are totally unaware of their negative behaviors.

If you surround yourself by downers, they will pull you down, or you will jump down to join them. Alternately, identify the individuals that always make you feel better, who smile, laugh, and are positive. They can be just the tonic you need to cure your down days.

Positive interactions with others can also help us forget our own issues. Whether you call it a distraction or a cure, focusing thoughts on someone or something else can help you manage the feelings brought on by depression.

Whether your triggers are people, places, or situations, preparation and knowing how deescalate your mind and body when your system goes into overdrive can help you avoid triggers and minimize depressive episodes.

Use a simple self-awareness tool to give you control and help you avoid triggers.

Anxiety Self-Analysis:

1) **Identify 1-10, how bad is your anxiety? (For levels over 3, follow all steps.)**

2) **A. Evaluate your surroundings.**

    (1) Are there specific objects/people/factors in the immediate area that make you nervous, stressed, or uncomfortable?

    (2) Can you eliminate the negative influences from your surroundings?

    (3) Do you need to leave the room?

    (4) What/who is around that could help?

B. Make a change in your environment. (See 2.B. below)

3) **A. Focus on your physical body.**

    i) Is your heart racing?

    ii) Are you having difficulty breathing?

    iii) Are you chilled or having sudden hot flashes?

    iv) Are you shaking, tremoring, dizzy or faint?

    v) Is your stomach cramping?

B. Perform breathing exercises. (See next page)

C. Practice self-talk. (See chapter on changing your brain)

4) **A. Focus on your senses.**

    b) What are your favorite smells?

    c) Sounds?

    d) Materials or fabrics?

    e) Pictures?

    f) Tastes?

    g) Sights?

    h) What makes you feel happy?

B. Participate in a sensory experience that calms you.

Create a habit of doing a self-anxiety exam several times a day, or until you learn to recognize when your anxieties are strong enough to trigger negative behaviors and thoughts. If you realize you need action to calm or change you situation, try the following activities:

2. B. Environmental Changes

- Walk into a different room.
- Remove a negative object or reminder.
- Go outside. Focus on nature, like the breeze, moon, rain, fresh air, etc.
- Leave the situation or ask an unwanted "guest" to leave.

3.B. Breathing Exercises

- Close your eyes and breathe in four counts through your nose and out four counts through your mouth. Repeat for 3-4 minutes.
- Place your first two fingers on your forehead and use your thumb to cover one nostril. Lean your head slightly forward and breathe in through a single nostril and out through your mouth. (This limits air intake and slows breathing and heart rate.)
- Sip air slowly, (like using a straw), and breathe out your nose.
- Put your hand on your diaphragm (below your ribs). Breathe in and out through your nose, inflating your stomach like a balloon. Inhale four counts, exhale four counts.

4.B. Sensory Experiences

- Spray a calming scent or candle
- Smell the flowers and plants near you
- Cuddle with your favorite blanket
- Pet or cuddle with an animal
- Listen to water (turn on the faucet)
- Yoga or other stretching
- Take a shower or bath; wash your hair and body
- Give or get a massage or pedicure
- Look at your favorite artwork or photos
- Enjoy a favorite food or flavor
- Take your shoes off and walk in the grass
- Think of or look at the mountains, lake, forest, or other calming place in nature

PRESS ON.

Quick Trigger Can-Do Tips:

- Keep a daily journal of your moods and activities. Analyze it to look for patterns.
- Ask a friend or loved one to help identify your triggers. Others may be able to see habits or patterns you cannot see.
- Look for pick-me-ups that help you and let go of the stresses of life.
- Don't go there. (There includes any mental place or physical situation that you KNOW is not good for you.)
- Plan ahead. Expect delays, crowds, or construction zones of all kinds. Mentally prepare for what is to come.
- Recognize situations common for causing anxiety or triggering feelings of self-doubt:

  - Loss of control
  - Loss of a loved one
  - Transition (school, aging, marriage, divorce)
  - Financial stress
  - Abuse
  - Conflict
  - Social gatherings
  - New places
  - Crowds
  - Sleeplessness
  - Traveling woes/unknowns
  - Unexpected encounters
  - Competition
  - Deadlines
  - Unexpected decisions
  - Long car rides
  - Traffic
  - Stress
  - Speed
  - Grief
  - Being late
  - Tests or performances
  - Inadequacy
  - Hospitals
  - Health concerns
  - Disappointment
  - Job interviews or evaluations
  - Changes in your routine
  - Unfamiliar people
  - Temperature
  - Altitude
  - Changes in barometer
  - Smells
  - Storms

CHAPTER 7:
Self-Care

When life presses down on you, it can require all your time, effort, and energy to hold your ground. During these times, we can find ourselves just trying to keep our heads above water. We often neglect everything but the most essential. Sometimes this means we neglect even the basics of caring for ourselves (and at times, our family members).

If someone disappears from life, there is a reason. When we are drowning in a terrible whirlpool of depression, the last person we care about is oneself. Missy* faded from the presence of the world; several days passed before her friend, Deann, noticed her absence and called. Missy tearfully choked out a few sentences on the phone.

> "I haven't showered in three days. I've barely even left my room. The only food I have is Gatorade, but even that is now making me sick. Since my roommate is out of town, and I don't have a job, I haven't even talked to a real person in days.
>
> I can't sleep at night, so I try to read or watch TV, but I can barely even focus. When I do fall asleep, usually sometime in the early morning, I toss, turn, and wake up sick and still not feeling rested. There's just no point."

Though she didn't say it at the time, she later indicated she had also been consuming alcohol and other numbing substances.

Miles away, there was little Deann could physically do for Missy, other than listen. After hearing the desperation of the situation,

Deann realized her friend needed an immediate goal, some area to focus on with small, but achievable steps that would help her feel better. Considering the state her friend was in, Deann realized the first thing Missy needed to do was to take care of herself, to meet the physical demands of her body.

> "As silly as it sounds, I had to walk her through the steps. I told her that as soon as we got off the phone, she needed to go take a bath, wash her face and hair, and then get dressed. She hadn't eaten either, so we talked about what food she had in the apartment and what she should eat to help her feel better. It was awful to know she was in such a bad place, but I was glad to find out later that our conversation was the encouragement she needed to take care of herself." – Deann Bingham

> "When our bodies aren't being taken care of, our minds will follow suit. Physical inactivity is as bad for the brain as the body. "I learned a long time ago that I need to get ready as soon as I get up. Showering and getting dressed is a signal to my mind and body that it is time to do something. Especially when I am depressed or anxious, I need the physical change to spark mental change. If I don't get ready when I first wake up, it is far too easy to crawl back in bed, nap on the couch, or sit around all day in my pajamas. When I get dressed and ready for the day, I am much more likely to get out of my apartment and do something." – Andrea Lofthaus

For some, self-care is just the opposite of getting dressed and ready for the day. It may mean staying in pajamas and taking a break from the norm to take time for themselves.

> "When I had depression, I couldn't be sociable. I drifted through six months, which I remember very little about other than the daily struggles; such as how difficult it was to make my son's packed lunch because my hands felt numb and heavy. When I was left with anxiety rather than full on depression, I found that a change of scene helped. I needed a quiet space or a quiet walk. Mindfulness helps me the most. When I'm on the edge of tipping back into depression, I have to stop, take a day off, and do nothing. That pulls me back into an okay-frame of mind." – Karen Johnson

Though it may seem trite to remind yourself, or someone you love, to "take a shower" or "eat breakfast" or "take time for yourself," even life basics can fall away when someone is overwhelmed in a battle for survival.

Long-time sufferer Kathy Wade recalls the best advice given to her. "It is okay to be selfish to take care of yourself."

If you find yourself, or someone you love, in an all-consuming struggle, encourage basic hygiene and self-care activities to help cleanse the body and mind.

Self-care isn't selfish.
It is a priority and necessity, not a luxury.

PRESS ON.

Quick Self-Care Can-Do Tips:

- Take a shower or bath.
- Wash your hair.
- Eat. (Do not consume fast food or preservatives, as these trigger headaches and gut issues, which increase depression. Basics like oatmeal, fruit, vegetables or nuts boost a body that it has been deprived.)
- Drink a glass of water. (Actually, drink several.)
- Wash your face.
- Apply moisturizer to your skin or face.
- Brush your teeth.
- Get dressed.
- Change your clothes.
- Brush your hair.
- Make your bed. (This serves multiple purposes. Once made, it is less likely that you will get back in your bed, and it will get you moving, as well as create peace and organization in the space.)
- Do a load of laundry.
- Go for a walk, do sit-ups, walk up and down stairs, or engage in an activity that forces you to move your body (even cleaning your home or making the bed).
- Trim and clean your nails.
- Shave.
- Do your hair, make-up, or other personal practice that helps you feel a little better or freshen up.

CHAPTER 8:
Healthy and Happy

Stephen R. Covey taught that one of the most critical steps for success is to "sharpen the saw." He said, "Sharpen the Saw means preserving and enhancing the greatest asset you have—you."

The more care we extend to our bodies, the *better* they will perform and the *longer* they will perform well.

People hate that food and exercise are answers to nearly every physical problem, but the body speaks truth, even if we choose to ignore it. Study after study demonstrates the importance of living a healthy lifestyle, one that includes basic exercise and plenty of natural foods, plants, veggies, fruits, and berries. Going back to nature can be part of the solution for depression for multiple reasons.

NUTRITION
by Rebecca Clayson

Good nutrition nourishes the body and brain, making our minds stronger to deal with difficulty. Some foods, such as chocolate, breads, and sweets, produce a temporary lift from the simple carbs, and then create a drop in mood when blood sugar falls. Use these sparingly. Water is an essential nutrient for the body and especially the brain.

In the article, "Why Your Brain Needs Water," Joshua Gowin, PhD, states, "Of all the tricks I've learned for keeping my mind sharp...staying hydrated may be the one I follow most closely. Our brains depend on proper hydration to function optimally. Brain cells require a delicate balance between water and various elements to operate, and when you lose too much water, that balance is disrupted."

It makes sense, then, that adequate water helps combat the chemicals that get off and lead to depression and anxiety. So drink up! A poor diet prohibits the body from absorbing and using the beneficial foods, minerals, and nutrients we take in.

HEALTH AND WELLBEING

Illness and disease alter the normal state of the body, which can trigger depression. When a system is faced with survival mode from a long- or short-term illness, the brain reroutes all resources to fight the foreign cell invaders, the germs, or the problem at hand. This can cause a change in metabolism, energy, chemical balance, hormone levels, and adrenal functioning, any of which can trigger depression.

The condition of the physical body is closely and carefully linked to wellbeing and mental health. Nearly all cancer patients, for example, also struggle with depression at some time.

When the physical body is in decline, mental health often follows suit. Sometimes it is a semi-conscious choice: as we dwell on our inabilities or illnesses, we can feel like we will never be well, or we lose our sense of personal value because we aren't able to *do* as much as we could in our healthier lives. This mindset is a one-way train to despair.

The Family Guidance Center for Behavioral Healthcare says, "The connection between mental health and physical health is strong. And just as chronic illness may lead to depression, depression can deepen the symptoms of physical illness."

Julie* suffered from debilitating daily depression for more than a decade before she found the right help to turn her life around.

> "My children were little and I got stuck in an unhealthy series of habits. My husband worked all the time, and I was practically a single mom to five small kids. I feasted on junk because I thought it fulfilled some emotional need I had. Candy and packaged 'treats' consumed me, and I consumed

them. They made me feel better for a moment, and so I kept repeating the cycle because I hoped those moments would last longer and fill the emptiness I felt inside."

For years, Julie retreated from the world. She discontinued activities she once loved, including involvement in her kids' school and going to church.

"I didn't feel good enough to sit in church. Looking around, I thought everyone else was perfect and I was broken. I couldn't bring myself to go, even though it had always been a place of hope and support.

"When I finally sought help, I told the doctor that something was wrong with me. I had him test me for all sorts of problems and diseases, and the tests kept coming back as normal. At one point, I looked at him and said, 'Don't you dare tell me I have depression. I know I am depressed, but there has to be a cause.' Initially, he wanted to put me on an anti-depressant. I know there can be benefits to that, but I also knew that the years-long cycle I was in would never break if I didn't change myself fundamentally on the inside."

What Julie discovered was a breakdown in her digestive system. Her candy addiction had zapped her body of nutrients and even the ability to use good food she ingested. For her, the recovery process included reprogramming her body and changing her mentality about food, health, and her mental and physical control of herself.

"Some people don't want to hear it, but I had to completely clean out my digestive system and start again. Slowly, I developed better eating habits. Mostly I stopped consuming sugar and I started eating greens, lots of vegetables, fruit, and fresh foods. Now I eat produce I grow in my garden, so I have a lifelong love and hobby, as well as improved health and more control over my mental swings and shifts."

Interestingly, Julie now sees her own daughter following in her unhealthy pattern of consuming sugar, sweets, and all processed foods.

"Not long ago, I pulled my daughter aside and told her, 'We are related, you know, you are prone to experience the same problems I faced, and that is a path you don't want to go down.'"

While Julie acknowledges that depression is not always as "simple" as changing your diet, it is a trigger and often goes unidentified by those caught in the cycle.

• "When I find myself falling into depression, not just having a bad day or experiencing the natural ups and downs of life, but really falling; I stop and take a deep look at my life. Most of the time I realize that because I was stressed or something else had my attention, I started cheating on myself and eating poorly again. My physical health always impacts my mental health."

Not all personal experiences are as clearly linked to personal health as Julie's story, but health is a definite contributor, either for good or ill.

"When I eat high-fat, high-calorie, high-carbohydrate foods, I feel foggy and lethargic. When I eat proteins, fruits and vegetables and complex carbohydrates, I can think more clearly. Knowing this fact, however, doesn't always make my food choices simple. Sometimes I simply don't care." – Camille Ballou

Sometimes, as Camille notes, we just don't care. When individuals are in the throes of depression, they often have little desire or energy to eat well. They don't bother to cook, or sometimes to eat at all.

Krystal lived off of energy drinks for days until she became so sick she could barely function. Casey ate packaged food all the time, the perfect snack for a busy student—until his digestive system stopped breaking down preservatives and he ended up in the hospital. Samuel worked daily to prove that men can live on bread alone, but it created a glut in his intestines and he wound up in the E.R. with pain, cramping, inability to have a bowel movement and nausea. Coincidence?

As a college student, John Marler drank soda for the caffeine and sugar so he could make it through long days and nights. He peaked at drinking more than two gallons of soda a day. When he tried to wean himself off, his body fought back, first by causing severe shaking and tremoring, following by vomiting, and eventually his system started shutting down and he wound up in the hospital for days. His addiction to soda spiraled him into depression so severe it nearly took his life.

> "Talk about a wake-up call. At first the soda was keeping me going during the day and helping me pull all-nighters in the name of studying for classes. But the more I drank, the more I had to have. My friends noticed and many playfully teased me about it. I didn't think much about it until it turned into an all-consuming addiction." — John Marler

After leaving the hospital with a new and careful eating plan, John began to rebuild his body and regain his health—and his emotional wellbeing.

> "I don't think my struggle with depression will ever be over, but at least now I feel like I have the upper hand. Or at least I know what I do and what I eat contributes to how I feel. And now I am a father. I want to be healthy and set a good example for my young daughter, and I want to be present for my wife—and my life. I want to be okay, and now I know how."

John's college experience is not an anomaly. Take the phrase "the freshman fifteen"; it is more than a stereotype, it is a truth. When we *indulge* in the merries of food and drink, we forget that our health habits impact our bodies.

One problem is that most of us don't truly understand the physiological and chemical processes taking place within our bodies; therefore, we don't really know how to best fuel them. But the truth is, you don't have to know it all to get the gist of it.

People with depression often have worse physical health, as well as worse self-perceived health, than those without depression. *Poor physical health brings an increased risk of depression.*

The jury is in. Take care of your body before it stops taking care of you.

Need a simple way to start? Try the researched advice of Michael Pollan: "Eat food. Not too much. Mostly plants."

PRESS ON.

Quick Can-Do Health Tips:

- Add green plants to your diet.
- Cut back on the intake of soda and other sugary or unnatural drinks.
- Limit your caffeine intake to under 400 mg a day.
- Eat a salad every day (skip the dressing; go for salsa or lime juice instead).
- Go for a brisk walk.
- Get in the sunshine for at least 5 minutes a day.
- Avoid chemical sugar substitutes (especially aspartame, Equal, NutraSweet, saccharin, sucralose, and high fructose corn syrups of any kind).
- Drink more water. Don't think you can drink a gallon of water a day? Start by increasing consumption by a cup a day. Tea and other water-based drinks count, so drink up.
- Eat 2-3 servings of fruit or berries a day.
- Drink freshly made fruit and veggie juice.
- Eliminate foods high in preservatives.

CHAPTER 9:

Expect Imperfection

"Disappointment is a sort of bankruptcy—the bankruptcy of a soul that expends too much in hope and expectation." This quote by Eric Hoffer defines the frustrations of millions living in first-world countries for whom the relative ease of life has spiked a dramatic rise in expectations. It is no longer enough to be satisfied with a place to call home and food on the table. We expect instantaneous response, regardless of circumstances.

Research has shown that our levels of life satisfaction are often associated with how any given experience compares to our expectations of the event or individual. This explains why a movie you've never heard of, and therefore have no expectations of, can be a surprise hit. The key is the surprise. When the forecast is for stormy weather, sun lovers are pleasantly surprised and very satisfied by rays of light streaming from the sky, but a planned sunny day, with the same results, may bring lower levels of satisfaction because the individual simply got what they expected.

Consider the irony of the following situation. An advertisement for a remote cabin in the woods of Montana touted the seclusion and quiet of the wilderness. Visitors were told to expect regular wildlife guests, including deer and foxes that come within feet of the large viewing deck. The cabin had all the basic amenities for spending a relaxing week in the forest. However, guests left the following poor reviews:

> "There was only one channel of ESPN and I couldn't watch the big game. Come on, get with the times!" -- Guest, May 2017

"The Wi-Fi wouldn't work in all areas of the cabin and when I called the owners for them to fix it, I didn't even receive a return call for a day." - - Guest, June 2017

Have we become so dependent on the "cloud" that we base our happiness on receiving every wish and whim of our thoughts?

"When I was pregnant, I read an informative book called *What to Expect When You're Expecting*. It was incredibly helpful in understanding what was going on in my body, and how the baby within me was developing. When my oldest child was born, I purchased the next book, *What to Expect the First Year*. While the information was just as informative, suddenly I had a marker for everything my son did. The first time he crawled should have been wonderful, except that I knew he was already a late crawler, according to the average timeframe for infant crawlers.

After a few milestone moments turned into comparative disappointments, I finally closed the book once and for all. Joy comes from feeling satisfied, and I discovered I am more able to find joy and happiness when I truly live my own experiences—not live them in comparison to the experiences of another." -- Jodi Orgill Brown

Similarly, comparing ourselves to others can give us unhealthy benchmarks. Consider the perspective shared by this author and long-time depression sufferer.

"It is insanely difficult to make myself go anywhere when I'm depressed. It means taking a shower, which uses more energy that I almost can't handle. It puts me on odd footing before I even step out the door with no makeup and well-worn clothes. The most challenging bit is the never-ending chant that echoes through my head: 'Not good enough. Not good enough. NotGoodEnough.' It drowns the voices of those around me and has me fighting tears before anyone approaches. Almost I leave. Every single time I go out when depressed, I almost leave for the safety of home . . . but I don't. I stay, suffering and deaf from the voices in my head, and hope I can connect to someone. Anyone. I keep my head bowed and watch the floor and the many shoes. The shoes somehow become more important than the feet or the person wearing them. I just watch those shoes and if they stop at me, I look up. Does it help when I force myself to be social? Yes and no. I'm almost always glad I went, but I never really connect, which can deepen the depression when I realize the voices were right. It's a battle." -- Karen Gillespie Hoover

Anytime we compare ourselves to a perceived "normal" (which we feel we are not), we risk feeling worse and falling deeper into depression. Not good enough is a lie — and a comparison.

> "Part of my fight was realizing that I was good enough. I forced myself to go out when I DIDN'T have all the trappings I felt were absolutely necessary. The whole, 'I must shower every day even if I'm not dirty or smelly,' 'I have to wear makeup or else I'm ugly,' 'I have to wear nice clothes to be acceptable outside my home,' and 'I have to do my hair nice to be acceptable,' those are all feeding the 'I'm not good enough' mantra. But, you ARE good enough, even without makeup or nice hair or nice clothes or a shower, and you don't even have to do those things every single day to be acceptable to those who love you. Once you toss that lie that you must meet certain physical criteria, it's easier to go out and see the love there for you and that you can give perfectly well AS YOU ARE." – Dyany Dittmer Munson

When we compare ourselves to others, we are often expressing feelings of perceived and real self-imperfection. These expectations can be even harder to let go of because they are ingrained in our minds—not because they are true, but because we have told ourselves lies for so long, some part of us believes the destructive fiction.

The myth of perfection has murdered dreams, ideas, relationships, and lives. It cannot be found in magazine pages, on porn sites, with the other woman, in a fast car, with a skin product, or from the quarterback, missionary, or cheerleader. Only when we let go of our own expectations of ideal can we embrace the messy ups and downs of truly beautiful lives.

Realizing we don't have to "have it all" or "be it all" to be happy can actually increase our tendency to experience satisfaction in life and deal more effectively with our lows.

Sri Sri Ravi Shankar, founder of the Art of Living spiritual movement, believes the consumer culture doesn't help, "When…life seems to have no aim and meaning, then people do get depressed, despite having so many physical comforts."

The strong pull toward consumerism does trick people into believing things will make them happy, which is a proven falsehood. No matter how many endorphins are released with the purchase of the newest item trending online, once the adrenaline rush is over, you and I are no happier than before the purchase. (Additionally, this contributes to the addictive side of shopping, as some people get caught in the physiological response, which wears off. Like a drug, they seek for the high of the experience again and get caught in the cycle of buying for the rush of the sale instead of actual improvements to lifestyle from the purchase.)

Couples therapist Esther Perel concludes that unrealistic expectations doom relationships. She notes that no single person can be *everything*: play the role of the best friend and confidante, as well as the lover, the dependable partner and the spontaneous adventurer. When one or both partners assume the relationship will provide for all of their social needs, the once-happy union unravels.

How can we overcome the burdens of unrealistic expectations? Expect imperfection. The burger will rarely compare to the ad photo and your date may burp or talk with his mouth open—but these "flaws" are merely a glimpse at real life.

Not only should we not expect self-perfection, we will be more content and more open to others when we drop the myth of perfection and embrace the scars of life.

"Toss the lie; live the truth. Embrace imperfection."
-- Sandi Rytting

PRESS ON.

Quick Can-Do Tips to Embrace Imperfection:

- Acknowledge pleasant surprises. List them in a notebook, to a friend, or in a prayer.
- Plan for traffic. Leave 10 minutes early. (And enjoy a few extra minutes to read if you arrive before your appointment.)
- Disconnect from social media.
- Go to the store before you get ready for the day. (And notice that people will still help you, talk to you and serve you, without makeup on or your hair done.)
- Make a habit of noting all the things that went right in your day.
- Embrace scars. (Scars signify growth after a struggle.)
- Read memoirs. (Memoirs usually include hard-learned lessons from imperfect events/characters).
- Unfollow social media stars who misrepresent their lives as perfect or always on vacation.
- Carry batteries or chargers. Prepare for the normal drain and strain of life.
- Don't follow news events—media covers crises, emergencies and the worst of what is happening in the world.
- Leave your phone at home.
- Read descriptions of movies rather than watch trailers, which just serve to increase the hype and expectations.

CHAPTER 10:
Turning Outward

Giving to others jump-starts a healthy life. As soon as your service pebble hits the water and ripples into the world, you feel the intrinsically satisfying joy that comes from doing good.

Time Magazine writer Jenny Santi says, "Altruism is hardwired in the brain—and it's pleasurable. Helping others may just be the secret to living a life that is not only happier but also healthier, wealthier, more productive, and meaningful."[ix]

> "'Lose yourself in the service of others.' That is a message I hear from my church leaders all the time. We don't think of getting lost as a good thing, but when we are in the throes of depression, then getting lost, or separated from our thoughts, is good. When I am thinking about other people, when I am helping someone else, then I am not focused on myself. Even a few minutes of focusing on others puts my life in perspective.
>
> It brings me happiness knowing I am putting a smile on someone else's face. In fact, I think it makes me just as happy as the person receiving the service." – Tami O. Baker

Turning toward others doesn't have to take a lot of effort, but it returns tenfold.

> "I started working night shifts because I couldn't handle the long hours of dark by myself. The days alone were still hard, but not as bad as the nights. I didn't start to get a handle on my depression until I followed the advice of a respected friend. The advice? Help others.
>
> When I started looking for friends, or strangers, who might need my help, I was surprised by how much I could do for others. Now I know that there are other people who need me as much as I need them. For all my

lonely days, there are hundreds, if not thousands of others who feel the same way, and the crazy thing is, we all think we are alone!

Getting involved with others made me temporarily forget myself. There is no 'cure' for depression, but helping someone else can be a lifesaver, for the giver and the receiver." -- John T.

If you want a fast way to get yourself out of the funk you are in, start by thinking about someone else. But don't stop with thinking, follow through and do something.

"You can sit there and think about helping all day long, but you actually have to do it. Until you act on your good intention, it is not going to benefit you or the other person.

The key is remembering to do it when you are bad; that is when you need it the most, but also when it is the hardest to do." – Tami O. Baker

How can a struggle as deep and all encompassing as depression be even briefly relieved by such small acts? Those who struggle with depression feel deeply. We, therefore, can also imagine the feelings of others, and that seed of thought, that someone else might be suffering, can motivate us to relieve their pain.

"The one thing I can always count on to help me feel better is doing service for someone else. If I know someone needs help and I can focus on someone else, that is what helps my depression more than anything." – Kendra Miller

Turning outward can also result in relationships, not just volunteer hours.

"I am always strengthened through serving others—and we form beautiful friendships and spiritual bonds that last forever." – Alesia Budd

When we acknowledge our own need for relief, that thought can be a prompt, a positive trigger, to consider similar needs of another.

"I love the thought that when I am helping someone else, it may be relieving some of their stress. Through little things, like mowing a lawn or giving a neighbor child a ride, I am bringing happiness to others.

One underlying key for resolving depression is getting outside of yourself. There is a reason you hear it all the time; it really works. When you are focused on yourself you see from one perspective: how bad things are, the woes of the world, or how you wish you could change things. But when you focus outside of yourself, it brings a sense of comfort you can't get anywhere else." – Tami O. Baker

Even the very source of your most painful days can be a gift to someone else, if you let it.

"Interestingly, my depression has caused many of my best qualities to grow and to flourish. Though I will not pretend to be the nicest or most considerate person in the world, I have found I have an insatiable need to help people who feel down or who are having problems." – Brandon T. Orgill

Taking that first step toward helping someone else isn't as difficult or overwhelming as it feels when you are suffering, alone and feeling hopeless. In the dark recesses of our minds, despair traps us into believing we are not good enough to help another. If we cannot even function ourselves, how could we possibly have anything to contribute to someone else? That is a flat-out lie. It is a deception we tell ourselves, or perhaps someone else has told us, but it is wrong, in every way.

Whether or not you believe in the *dark side of the force*, certain falsehoods circulate in society, and often settle in our minds when we are most vulnerable.

"When I was in college, I took a few years sabbatical and served a service and humanitarian mission for my church. The whole point of the mission was to put away my own desires and needs and serve God by helping other people. I am from a small town and had only traveled a few hundred miles from my home in my whole life, when I was sent to South America.

The first shock (besides culture shock) was that I fell into a deep depression. My whole life I'd planned the experience, but I got there and felt completely alone and inadequate.

I lived with another couple of guys who were also serving missions. They seemed to enjoy their experiences, but I felt like a complete failure. How could I help others when I could barely speak Spanish, I couldn't stomach the food, and I woke up everyday feeling like I was stuck in a bad dream?

It didn't take long to feel humbled. I started praying, but I wondered if God even remembered me. But me and my missionary buddies saw a little kid on the street. He was by himself, carrying an old deflated soccer ball. I still couldn't say much, but I said, 'Jugar?,' the Spanish word for play. His face lit up and he dropped the flat ball to the ground and kicked it to me. It was the best soccer game I've ever played. We didn't keep score, but I know we all won that day.

That was the first time I knew that I was in the right place. It wasn't about me and how awful or inadequate I felt, it was about that little kid, and all the other kids like him who just needed someone to care." – *B.H.

You have something to offer the world, and if it changes only one life for one minute, that is enough.

"I am part of several online forums for people with depression. One time, a woman from one of the groups sent me an email and asked for help, said she was losing hope. We didn't know each other, but somehow she decided to ask me. I debated if I *could* respond (I never questioned if I *should* respond, only if I could). I knew I lacked the know-how to help myself and I doubted if I could do anything to help her. But the fact that she asked a stranger—well, it made me guess she was desperate. I replied with a brief note and a link to a catchy song. That's it. But, it turned out, she just needed someone to care enough to reply. And I did. And we are both better for it." – Dee*

TURNING INSIDE OUT INTO A HABIT

When your mind turns your bed into a cage or your walls into a jail cell, it can be hard to imagine a reason or way to escape. You can begin to feel as if depression is a physical prison, holding not just your mind, but also your body. Breaking out may seem impossible, but you can still find ways to turn outward.

"More than down in the dumps, I was totally depressed. The long winter days had taken a toll on me mentally, and my only-sometimes-functional body had further sent me into a whirlpool. I felt alone, without purpose, overwhelmed—and too embarrassed to admit any of it. So, when the phone rang, I didn't answer, even though what I probably needed most was interaction with someone who cared.

I buried myself under my covers for a few hours, and then I tucked myself in a corner chair with a book, anything to avoid the painful feelings I had about life. Several days turned into weeks. Each day after the kids left for school, the scenario replayed.

My mind, it seemed, wouldn't allow me to be happy. I wondered if it was hormones, an early mid-life crisis, or even just a bad mood that had become a bad mode. At times, I perked up for hours here and there, especially when my family was around, but for the most part, I just didn't know how to get out of the funk I was in.

One particularly bad day, I'd climbed back in bed as soon as the kids were off. Hours passed and I felt again like I was simply not enough. Then my phone buzzed. A message. I almost didn't get up to look at it, but I took a chance.

The text was short, but it offered me escape from the darkness. In that moment, I knew someone was thinking about me. Someone cared. My friend texted just to check in and say hi, but that day, she saved me. Not from physical death, but from feelings of hopelessness that threatened to drown my soul.

Weeks later, it was my turn to help a friend. I thought about Teri* constantly and I figured if I texted her even a fraction of the times she was on my mind, she would feel my concern and know she was not alone.

I started by texting a smiley face, heart, flower, balloon, or high-five sign. Something so little, but that was all it took to let light into our lives. I say 'our' because I thought it was a way for me to help her, but it changed both of us.

Our friendship and trust grew with every emoji tear and every real tear. It was a way to express hurt and sorrow without the fear of rejection or negative feedback. She validated me and loved me, no matter what I was going through. We learned that our raw feelings were safe with each other—and we realized we weren't the only ones who struggle." – Jodi Orgill Brown

We all need to feel loved and remembered. At times we are on the receiving end of these sentiments, but giving them is just as critical for our emotional and mental survival.

One good way to form a habit of turning outward is to schedule it. Habituate your actions by making them a regular part of your routine. Make a concentrated effort to go twenty-eight days in a row, and you will officially be turned inside out.

"Forget yourself and go to work."
-- Bryant S. Hinckley

PRESS ON.

Quick Can-Do Tips for Turning Outward:

- Use commute time as time to talk on the phone to a friend or visit with the person next to you on the subway.
- Look people in the eyes. Return their gaze with a smile.
- Send a heart or smiley face text to three people every day.
- Walk out of your office and talk to the first person you see.
- Pay for the drink of the person behind you in line.
- Ask a simple question: "Is there anything I can do for you?"
- Practice seeing the people around you (not hoping they don't see you).
- Leave a handful of pennies at the store checkout lane.
- Don't look down. Look up.
- "See a need, fill a need." (From the animated film, "Robots.")
- Enlist the help of neighborhood children and find a yard or house that needs work, and then volunteer to help.
- Get in the habit of doing little things that focus on the greater good: pick up trash, pull a few weeds, move a tree limb, wave or smile as you pass others.

CHAPTER 11:
The Power of Gratitude

Have you wondered if gratitude is a true path to happiness, or just a fad? Fortunately, the power of gratitude is documented in multiple forms, all of which come to a similar conclusion:

The active practice of gratitude is transformative.

Benefits of Gratitude (from the Huffington Post and Forbes)

- Improved physical, emotional, and social wellbeing
- Greater optimism and happiness
- Improved feelings of connection in times of loss or crises
- Increased self-esteem
- Heightened energy levels
- Improved sleep
- Strengthened heart, immune system, and decreased blood pressure
- Improved emotional and academic intelligence
- Expanded capacity for forgiveness
- Decreased stress, anxiety, depression, and headaches
- Improved self-care and greater likelihood to exercise
- Heightened spirituality—ability to see something bigger than ourselves
- Increased empathy and decreased desires for revenge and retaliation

The 23 benefits listed are the proven physical, mental, and psychological enhancements that stem from a gratitude mindset.

Study the list above. How many of the bullet point topics affect you when you have depression? Low energy? No self-esteem? Can't sleep? Don't want to be social? The connections between the life improvements from gratitude and the life improvements needed when battling depression are astounding.

"Gratitude is the most exquisite form of courtesy."
- Jacques Maritian, French Philosopher

Life happens to all of us. Some things we earn, some we are given, others we cause, and still others just fall into our laps. But the choice to actively find good is within our control—and it is life changing.

"The one thing that puts life in perspective is to really and truly recognize the things that I have to be grateful for. No matter how hard things are, gratitude shows me that the good always outweighs the bad.

When I get outside of myself and see what is around me, even if means seeing the difficult circumstances others are going through, then I recognize how good life is. Being genuinely grateful for what you have helps you press forward. Gratitude is a cure-all when we take the time to remember and focus on what is right, rather than on what is wrong." – Tami O. Baker

In Forbes magazine, Amy Morin wrote, "We all have the ability and opportunity to cultivate gratitude. Simply take a few moments to focus on all that you have—rather than complain about all the things you think you deserve." But having the ability to be grateful and implementing gratitude as a practice are not the same.

"When you're just trying to make it through the day, finding things to be grateful for can seem almost impossible, and even fake. You might not feel grateful for anything. That being said, gratitude is healing for the soul and brings a light of hope into your life that nothing else can.

Gratitude is easiest to incorporate in your life when you make it a habit as opposed to something you try to do when you're feeling blue. By seeking to find gratitude daily, you're building an anchor for yourself that you can fall back on during those really difficult days. Truly, some of the best things in life are the hardest." – Celeste Noland

Erin Grimley's battle with depression began as a child, after a family crisis led to forever-altered relationships. (To read more of Erin's story, go to the section on triggers.) In her search for happiness, Erin discovered the power of mindful gratitude.

> "I try to think about the things I'm grateful for on a daily basis and why I'm grateful for those things. *If* I do this, *then* I am more positive. I try to do it before go to bed, so if I've had a bad day I can go to bed with positive thoughts. There have been times that I have forgotten to do my 'Gratitudes,' and then I don't sleep very well and I am tired and cranky in the morning." – Erin Grimley

Erin has determined she experiences a positive correlation between gratitude and positivity. *If* I am grateful, *then* I am more positive.

In addition, Erin has established a routine (even times of the day) when she practices gratitude. That allows her to recognize variations in situations for which she is grateful. She identifies both big-picture and in-the-moment conditions that are ripe for appreciation.

> "I'm grateful for my kids. My kids are a huge reason why I am the way I am now. While I was in my black hole of despair or 'depression', I looked at my kids and thought, 'What on earth am I doing with my life? My kids need me. I can't go on like this.' That's when I decided to get help so I can be a good mom.

> "Honestly, I am even grateful that I hit rock bottom and got help, or I wouldn't have figured out who I am and how to deal with the inner demons. Yes, the demons are still there. They're just not as strong anymore, and I know how to keep them at bay. Every now and again they break the bonds that hold them back and attempt to drag me down into the depths of darkness. When that does happen, I put on good uplifting music and think of the things I am grateful for—or I just go buy some color and do my hair. That makes me feel happy.

> "So, I am grateful for my talent of doing hair and being able to make myself and others feels better about themselves. I could go on and on about gratitude and how it helps fight depression. I am grateful for life!" – Erin Grimley

Not all of us have vocations that help us feel good about helping ourselves and others, as Erin's passion for doing hair, but the exercise is the same:

- Think about and study gratitude.
- Explore your life and find things you can be grateful for.
- Look for the causes of your happiness and identify the roots of your feelings.
- Implement the if, then process into your life to track the effect of your gratitude.

As part of your gratitude practice, learn the art of giving genuine praise, which serves to compliment others as well as build trust. Overzealousness in showing gratitude results in giving compliments that both the giver and receiver know are insincere. A simple but true acknowledgment can boost both the giver and the receiver. Consider the difference between "Hey, uh, nice sweater" and "Thanks for ringing up my groceries today. I appreciate your help. Self-serve checkout cannot compete with real service."

The more you look for reasons to be grateful, the more you will find them. When finding them starts to come with ease, consider taking your actions to another level.

"Go twenty-four hours without complaining, not even once, then watch how your life starts changing," says life-long depression sufferer, international best-selling author and writing coach Angie Fenimore. (Read more from Angie in chapters one and four.)

> "It is amazing for me to see how hard [going twenty-four hours without complaining] is for most of us to accomplish. A man told me he made it twenty-three hours and asked, 'Is that good enough? Does it count?' I told him it is the mental process, more than the actual time that counts.
>
> One woman could not release the idea that she had every right to complain; some complaints are justified, like when people are cruel to you, etc. And perhaps there is validity in this idea. . . .
>
> But what I've found is people who have the least are often the people who are the most grateful for what they have.
>
> If you break your word and complain, then start over. Just start over with a new twenty-four hours. You can live your life complaining or you can

live your life choosing who you are going to be." – Angie Fenimore

Even if you are not convinced that the practice works, give it a try and test the theory for yourself.

"My friend gave me a gratitude journal for my birthday. For two days, I jotted a few ideas, but with minimal thought. The book then sat on a shelf for a year before I picked it up again. By then I was facing some struggles that had me trapped in feelings of hopelessness and feelings of frustration with those around me. It was just months before my fortieth birthday, and I felt like my life was in chaos. I lacked direction and I had no daily routine, which caused me to reinvent the wheel every day after my kids left for school.

Knowing I needed a major change, I chose a few things and created a morning checklist. That gratitude journal became my first activity, either when I woke up, or when I had a few moments alone after the kids left. At first my daily gratitude lists took several minutes to finish, but after a while, they became easier and easier. At night, I found myself mentally reviewing the day, knowing already what I would write the next morning.

I made a commitment to go four months with my new routine, which also included prayer and personal study time, but the practice continued until my 280-page journal was full and my heart was at peace. That is the power of gratitude." – Jodi Orgill Brown

PRESS ON.

Quick Gratitude Can-Do Tips:

- Start a gratitude journal. Record three things in it every day.
- Say "thank you" often—particularly to those who serve you.
- Notice things you normally take for granted (amenities like sheets, lights, sunglasses, or refrigeration).
- Write down what you appreciate about yourself.
- Flip a hardship into a grateful blessing. "I am sick, but I am thankful to have a bed to sleep in." "My boss gave me another dead-lined assignment today, but I'm grateful he trusts me to accomplish it." "Your thoughts were hard for me to hear, but I appreciate your honesty."
- Practice not gossiping, complaining, or judging others.
- Tell others you are grateful for them.
- Think of something that went well today and list a reason why. ("The server brought my favorite soda without asking what I wanted." Reason: "I am friendly and have gotten to know the staff—and I tip well.") *Suggestion by Catherine Price.
- Think of a moment when someone expressed gratitude for you. How did it make you feel?
- Savor a moment. Pick something small and just enjoy: a few extra minutes in the shower or the taste of your morning pick-me up drink are perfect ways to savor the start of the day. *Suggestion by Catherine Price.
- Create a gratitude affirmation. "I appreciate kindness and I acknowledge efforts made to treat me with love." (For more on affirmations, see Chapter Four.)
- Write a letter of thanks to someone who has made a difference in your life. Give it in person, if possible.
- Express gratitude at meals, both when you are alone or with loved ones.
- Express or show gratitude to your partner. Men particularly appreciate acknowledgments of respect and evidence they are needed. Women particularly appreciate expressions of love and praise of effort (especially when the results of that effort aren't obvious).

CHAPTER 12:
Connection to a Higher Power

The great questions of life sometimes stare us in the face, and other times, they fade to the background, but like a test on a distant date, the pressure of finding the answers never fully goes away until we gain the knowledge for ourselves.

A simple children's song answers questions that elude some people for their entire lives:

> My life is a gift; my life has a plan.
> My life has a purpose; in heav'n it began.
> My choice was to come to this lovely home on earth
> And seek for God's light to direct me from birth.
> -- Vanya Watkins

Much of the world believes in a higher power, a god—or gods—of the earth, but God is known by different names to different people: Abba, Yahweh, Elah, Brahman, Allah, Elohim, and Jesus Christ are just a few.

If you do not believe a higher power exists, this chapter alone is not likely to convince you. But if you ever wonder why you suffer, or feel you are flawed, unloved, unheard, or broken beyond repair, then take heart and read on. Life, yours included, is part of a grand plan initiated by the grandest planner. A higher power is aware of you and can give you strength. So look up.

"We're not so strong, God is strong," says Richie Norton, international bestselling author of *The Power of Starting Something Stupid*. "We're weak. You can handle the things that happen to you if you rely on God."[x]

And Richie, and his wife and co-author Natalie, are some who know challenges, including death, injury, loss, physical pain, and mental anguish. But they also know that a higher power guides, directs, and comforts them during the worst of times.

"It's not about what happens to us," says Richie. "It's about how we react to those things. We do not blame God. We put our faith in God and know that God wants the best for us."

But what if you don't know that God wants the best for you? What if you are disillusioned by religion or frustrated by your own feelings of doubt or guilt?

> "Some believe in a God; some don't. I have found that at some point, a depressed person has to come to the realization that they are powerless to overcome their illness on their own.
>
> A depressed or mentally ill person is no more at fault for their situation than someone with a non-lifestyle related cancer or Type 1 Diabetes. At some point the guilt and the burden of your illness has to be turned over to a higher power." – Camille Ballou (see Camille's essay in Part III)

The burden of depression adds a mental, and sometimes physical, weight to life. The more desperate you feel, the more important it is to know your purpose—the WHY behind who you are—and how to cope with struggles.

> "I prefer to think of depression as a kind of Gethsemane. Not that any of us would equate ourselves with Jesus Christ, but He took on Himself sorrows that weren't his own and was completely weighed down by them. He prayed for the bitter cup to pass, but it didn't; He had to 'drink' it and go on." – Rebecca Clayson (see Rebecca's essay in Part III)

The less control you have of your situation, the more important it is to have belief in something greater. Lori Conger, survivor of the Cokeville, Wyoming, bombing and long-time sufferer of PTSD and depression, emphasizes how her beliefs are critical for pressing on.

> "At times I know if I do not reach out for Divine help, I will lose myself to despair. And so I pray—no, I plead, I *beg* for God's mercy and grace, seeking for the peace only He can give. He rescues me time and time again as a sweet, undeniable calm settles over me and I am reminded

that things will be okay."

Lori acknowledges that belief in a higher power does not assuage all challenges, trials or questions of life.

"It's not like all of my problems immediately vanish; the pain is still there, as raw as ever, threatening to literally destroy me, but I begin to feel even the slightest bit of hope, and I have learned that hope is a life-saving feeling. " (see Lori's essay in Part III)

GLIMPSES OF LIGHT

Depression often sets in when unwanted situations press down on us. For P. Traegger*, this came from a debilitating but undiagnosed health challenge. He was tested to his core; he questioned his worth to his family, his value, and his purpose in life.

"The pain pushed me to mental places I'd never visited before. Then the doctors told me I was a hypochondriac, that I was creating an illness in my mind, that nothing was wrong with me. That's when I contemplated—no, I planned—scenarios for my death; situations that would hopefully allow my family to go on without me.

I look back now and I almost don't know how I got through it, but then I remember exactly how I got through. God wouldn't let me forget where I'd come from—from Him. He didn't suddenly take away the excruciating pain, but little by little, He led me to people who helped me find relief, first from the physical pain, and then from the mental anguish. Now it's hard for me to admit that I planned to leave my wife and children. I hope they never know how bad it got. The only time I can bear to think about it is when I see someone else in a desperate situation. Only then do I quietly pull them aside and say, 'God is there for you. Don't give up.'"

After Aubrey Loose experienced overwhelming postpartum depression, she found hope from glimpses into her future, glimpses of light from God.

"I often would just 'check out'. I remember more than once sinking into the couch. My body felt so heavy, like I was being pulled deeper and deeper into the cushion. I realized I could not for the life of me convince myself to get up, and I just started to sob. It took me a long time to convince myself to do anything. If I managed to do any one household chore (which now takes me maybe twenty minutes), it was a good day. I would tell my husband that I was tired to the core. My body and mind were so tired that my whole body hurt.

The only thing that got me through that time was the fact that I saw a light at the end. That was a huge blessing Heavenly Father gave me. My day could seem so bleak, but I could pray and see that light of: 'This will pass. It will come to an end.' So I kept pushing through even the darkest of days." – Aubrey Loose

Darkness is a familiar place to author and depression sufferer Kelly A. Parkinson. But a higher power gives her strength to walk forward and to hold onto the rope.

"Do you ever feel like you are standing on a precipice staring down into a dark watery abyss that pulls you toward it like a magnet? You're trying to hold back, but it's as if something has taken hold of your ankles and is dragging you slowly and surely to your doom. There's nothing to grab onto, nothing to stop the inevitable drop that is sure to come.

But what if there were an invisible rope and if you only reached up, you'd find it? Would you stretch out your hand in faith, hoping that your fingers will wrap around that rope? Or would you doubt, believing only what you see with your eyes, and fall into Shadow?

I have fallen into that dark abyss. I was drowning in depression and anxiety. I couldn't breathe; the darkness was too heavy, too thick. I lost hope, I lost myself.

I struggled for a long time, trying to keep my head above the water, until I realized I needed to believe someone was there to save me, someone I couldn't see, but only feel.

He gave me the rope.

A rope I came to realize was made from thousands of tiny threads—of prayers by me and on my behalf, of the priesthood, the words of the Prophets, Scriptures, good books, family, friends, and many more—all those threads were put here to save me.

He did not leave me comfortless—the good Shepherd was leading me along the entire time, I just had to remember to not let go of the rope." – Kelly A. Parkinson

Why is the rope so important? It means someone is on the other end, someone who is invested in you who won't let go. Just as the failing student excels under the tutelage of a caring and dedicated teacher, we too can claw out of the pit of depression when there is a greater force willing us to grab hold, strain with every muscle, and reach up. When we acknowledge that we've been given the rope, we begin to feel the efforts to pull us up, even as we struggle with the climb.

> "I can't even begin to tell how many times the Lord placed the exact person in my life to help me. It was only because I pushed myself, testing my faith and strength to trust in the Lord, that I realized I'm stronger than I thought." – Alesia Budd

Discovering we are strong only occurs when we discover we *need* extraordinary strength to go on.

> "When depression starts creeping in on me, even doing daily activities can become overwhelming. I was at a point years ago that was beyond rock bottom for me in every sense, and I didn't even know how I could have the strength to make it through the night. I didn't want to be alive anymore and prayed for strength to help me see myself and the strength to overpower this fear. I knew, with the Lord's help, that I was the only one that could make things better so I could heal.
>
> Through God's help, I have come to know my true self and have an understanding of what I need to get past the depression before it takes hold—and a big part of that is to be around people and find the beauty in the simple and smallest of things." – M. K.

Sometimes, depression hits us because we envisioned grown-up life to be smoother, more glamorous, or more comfortable. Who knew life could be so depressing?

When we acknowledge a higher power, we recognize all things, creatures, people, and outcomes have a higher purpose than we currently understand. Our lack of understanding can actually guide and comfort us in the worst times. Knowing there is a purpose, a plan and ultimately a REASON for all suffering creates a motivation outside any moment or circumstance. That is not to say that we have no choice, or that all suffering is condoned or enacted by a higher power. Individuals do—like it or not—have choice. This agency allows us to screw up, and even do what a higher power would not want us to do. However, in the mud and gunk of life, a seed of purpose can take root.

"Earlier in my life, when things were easier, I chose to try to figure out if God actually existed: I tested that idea and started to gain evidence that He did exist, and He loved me, and He is good. So as things got harder, I had that understanding to start with. It wasn't enough to get me through the hard times. But it WAS enough to have taught me that I could do more testing and see if God would get me through the hardships. It was enough that I could start with a little faith that the tough times would work for my good, instead of being all bad. That God was still in charge and had my back.

I saw that some trials, which I thought were awful and terrible and insufferable, actually helped to prepare me for harder trials up the road, making them more bearable.

I saw that, as I began to recognize and face my weaknesses and mistakes, it gave me more understanding and sympathy for the weaknesses and mistakes of others, allowing me to love them rather than always getting angry and judging them when their mistakes or weaknesses were different than mine or hurt me.

I saw that it was okay to not be perfect or have a perfect life, and that I could actually be happy even when things didn't go according to plan.

I saw that some things that look all bad are not really all bad, but have a purpose I hadn't thought of that is really very good. And everything has SOME good to it, even if it is just what you or others learn from it.

- I began to learn the value of diligence, hard work, and not quitting.

- I began to learn the value of forgiving others and forgiving myself.

- I began to be able to laugh more at myself when things went wrong and cry more with others when they hurt.

- I began to see that the events in this life are not as important or long lasting as we sometimes think they are, but our choices are everything.

- I saw that as I learned to make these choices that helped me be happier and stronger, the choices became easier to make.

- I saw that letting my weaknesses, trials, and struggles define me and my life was as restrictive and miserable as a prison, but if I instead learned to deal with them, and work with God on them, and accept and understand and utilize Christ's atonement on them, that I became freer and happier than I ever thought possible.

- And from all of these things, I began to really learn how much God and Christ actually DO love me and ARE there for me and DO turn all the things that happen to me for my good. ALL of them. Because in learning and testing these things (and it took many years, and I'm still not done), I am still collecting data on the original questions: does God exist and does He love me?

- The data is pretty consistent.

- He does." – Dyany Munson (see Dyany's essay in Part III)

Faith often requires us to look past the gloomy world around us and toward the heavens; it can mean stepping out of reality and into a state of peace, even amidst raging war. But therein lies the benefit. Being out of touch with reality can be a good thing. Knowing God means you have reasons to live and succeed that are not based on perceptions of reality or the mess of society.

FROM SUFFERING TO LIVING

Many people question why a higher power would allow suffering, sin, and devastation. Perhaps the times of falling acclimate us to resistance and teach us to live well, even with discomfort.

"One afternoon on the way home from a doctor's appointment, I was so frustrated and so done with my suffering that I was determined to kill myself, using the many medications my doctors had me on, when I got home. I had it all planned out, right down to another mom picking my son up from preschool and taking him home with her.

When I arrived home, I realized I had a phone number stuck in my head. I vaguely remembered passing a spiritual support center on my way home and realized the phone number I had in my head belonged to this center. Something stopped me from killing myself that day. Now I know it wasn't something, but someone: God. I told God I'd give Him another chance. . . . I'm not sure what He thought of that.

103

It took me a week, but I finally called the spiritual center. I spoke with the most wonderful person who prayed with me over the phone and gave me a little bit of hope. It took another week for me to visit the center. I met the most caring, loving, nonjudgmental people there. One woman sat with me, holding my hands and eventually holding me as I cried and cried. They prayed for me because I just wasn't capable of praying for myself. I couldn't believe my ears when the woman who held me invited me to her home for Bible study. She didn't even know me, and that just touched my heart so much.

I had allowed my diseases to keep me trapped in my house and I was just so lonely; I always felt so alone. I went to her home, and after a few weeks of attending the Bible study, she invited me to her church. That's something I loved so much about my new friend—she wasn't pushy, and her timing was gentle.

I started going back to church, where I found friendship and hope. Back at the spiritual center, I began attending their support group for people with chronic illness, as well as their weekly prayer hour. I was the youngest in the support group and through God, I was open to the wisdom and advice of the older participants. I remember one woman told me that we are Type A personalities in Type C bodies. Another woman counseled me to allow my illnesses to teach me how to be a human *being* instead of a human *doing*. The center's leader, a former hospice chaplain, taught me so much about God, about being angry with Him, about trusting Him and about being loved by Him. I learned how to accept my new normal.

Am I cured? No.

Am I healed? YES." – Amy Furr

THE EXCHANGE

To come to a place of peace, we must come to understand the trade-off of suffering in exchange for personal growth. Ask yourself: *Would I trade this hardship if it meant giving up the lessons or understanding I could gain from it?*

"Years ago, if you had asked me what traits and values I desired for my family, I'd have given you a long list I hoped to instill and teach. I wanted to raise my children to become faithful, kind, honest, independent, helpful, compassionate, thoughtful, and motivated individuals who contributed to their communities and made the world a better place.

At that time, I couldn't have imagined that my abilities as a mother would be compromised, that I would spend years suffering from seemingly endless migraines, dizzy spells, a brain tumor, multiple surgeries, hearing loss, and facial paralysis, followed by depression and anxiety.

In hindsight, I realize these very trials, which nearly took my life, also strengthened my family. How could I raise truly compassionate children without them understanding why compassion is needed? How could I have miracles and faith in my life without needing miracles?

The battles we faced together challenged us—we could either fall into hopelessness or develop the habits and characteristics that would strengthen us and bring us closer.

Now I can finally see. I see that my children are becoming the people I hoped they would become, but it is because of the hardships we've faced in life. My preference would be to be awake and helping my kids get ready and off to school every day, but my medical situation doesn't always afford such luxuries. But it is this very frustration that has helped them develop into independent, highly motivated, highly functioning young people. They get themselves up, showered, dressed, breakfasts and lunches made, and out the door to school, often before I am out of bed. It is not the route I would have chosen, but it is the path from which they have learned some of the most important traits my husband and I wanted to impart to them.

When I connect the dots, it is easy for me to see that God has been involved the whole time. He helped us with the big defeats and the small heartaches and everything in between. Faith kept us going when the world was crumbling around us. Now we know, with divine help, we can make it through anything." – Jodi Orgill Brown

Thirty years after the bombing which could have taken her life, Lori Conger still relies on her beliefs in God to keep her going.

"It is no secret that without my faith, my life would be very different. Perhaps I would not even still be here. I cannot say for sure, but what I can say for sure is that God's love is real, and it is the most powerful thing on earth."

PRAYERFULLY POWERFUL

Prayer is more than just communication; it is connection to a higher power, one that helps you find calm and answers. Numerous sufferers of depression believe their invocations and pleas to God, are key components to mental and spiritual survival.

> "In my experience, there is nothing that brings such immediate relief and freshens perspective quite like wrestling with my Maker in mighty prayer." – Lori Conger

> "God helps me know that I am not alone and that struggles are part of life, but I can do it!" – Cayson D.

> "Depression can turn me into a zombie for days, where I am stuck in a mental, physical, and spiritual stupor. But inevitably, when I turn to God, he always turns back and helps me. I don't know why I stay hidden inside myself for so long before I remember to pray. I guess I am still working on that." – Angela Linnebaugh

Lasting foundations do not blow into place with cool breezes, but are forged with blazing fires and hammered fiercely into shape. All of us face the heat of life, but with the help of a higher power, the heat purifies our hearts and forms us into something better than we were before.

WHAT GOD OFFERS

Still not sure where you stand? Consider a few sacred verses, from various religions, that demonstrate what followers believe a higher power gives to them.

Guidance

> Quran, Adh-Dhuha 93:7 "And he found you lost and guided you."

> Holy Bible (KJV), Matt 7:7 "Ask, and it shall be given you; seek, and ye shall find; knock, and it shall be opened unto you."

Strength and Answers to Prayers

> Holy Bible (KJV), Psalm 138:8 "In the day when I cried thou answeredst me, and strengthenedst me with strength in my soul."

Relief

Quran Ch 94:5-6 "So verily with the hardship there is relief, verily with the hardship there is relief."

Support and Protection

Book of Mormon, 2 Nephi 4:20 "My God hath been my support; he hath led me through mine afflictions in the wilderness; and he hath preserved me upon the waters of the great deep."

Provision of Needs

Talmud, Yalkut, Beshalah, 16 "The Lord stands behind our own endeavors, and as He provides for the raven in the field, He provides for man also."

All Things Made Possible

Holy Bible (KJV), Matt 19:26 "But Jesus beheld them, and said unto them, With men this is impossible; but with God all things are possible."

Healing

Holy Bible (KJV), Psalm 147:3 "He healeth the broken in heart, and bindeth up their wounds."

Power, Love, and a Sound Mind

Holy Bible (KJV), 2 Timothy 1:7 "For God has not given us a spirit of fear, but of power, and of love, and of a sound mind."

Never Alone

Quran 57:4 "...and He is with you wherever you are."

An Ally

Holy Bible (KJV), Exodus 14:14 "The LORD shall fight for you, and ye shall hold your peace."

Peace

Doctrine and Covenants 121:7 "My son, peace be unto thy soul; thine adversity and thine afflictions shall be but a small moment;"

Perhaps the old Christian hymn, "Be Still, My Soul," by Katharina von Schlegel says it best: "Be still, my soul: The Lord is on thy side; With patience bear thy cross of grief or pain. Leave to thy God to order and provide; In ev'ry change he faithful will remain. Be still, my soul: Thy best, they heav'n-ly Friend, Thru thorny ways leads to a joyful end."

Thorny ways do crisscross the path of life, but a higher power, indeed a heavenly friend, is on your side.

PRESS ON.

Quick Higher Power Can-Do Tips:

- Act as though you already believe. Do what you think you would do if you knew a higher power was at work in your life.
- Pray. Offer a vocal or silent heartfelt benediction.
- Read a religious text. Get a copy of the Holy Bible, the Torah, the Quran, the I Ching, the Book of Mormon, the Talmud, or the Bhagavad Gita and spend fifteen minutes a day reading and investigating these ancient, uplifting texts.
- Go to church. (Hartford Institute estimates there are roughly 350,000 religious congregations[xi] in the United States, so you should be able to find a religious gathering nearby.)
- Visit a religious website to learn about basic beliefs and doctrines.
- Experiment upon the word. Choose commandments or laws from the religious texts and act upon them and see if it makes a difference in your life.
- Ask a trusted friend. Think about someone you respect and invite them to share their beliefs with you.
- Commune with nature. Look at the world as a creation by a higher power and marvel at the variety and details of the creations.
- Visit a holy site. Find a local temple, mosque, church, or sacred site and invite the peace and holiness into your spirit.
- Change your environment. Go somewhere out of your norm and listen for the thoughts and ideas that come to you in a new place.
- Make a gratitude list. Think of a higher power as the source of goodness in your life.

CHAPTER 13:

Sleep

Many people struggling with depression find themselves sleepless and fighting against the darkness of the night. When the daylight breaks, restlessness and hopelessness often break and perhaps a few restful moments come.

Of the eighteen million Americans diagnosed with depression, more than nine million report regular insomnia. Is it any wonder that as a society we are becoming more depressed? Without adequate sleep, we can't rejuvenate our systems or think clearly.

For years it was believed that insomnia was a symptom of depression, but now research shows that insomnia may precede and/or cause depression. In many persons, it may even double the risk of depression.[11]

> "Sleep eludes me. Insomnia hunts me every night until I am sure the predator will capture, torture, and kill me. I can't even daydream about sleep.
>
> The battle has trudged on for so many years, I don't remember now if I stopped sleeping because of my depression, or if I got depressed because I wasn't sleeping. The lines blur, like my vision when I try to drink myself away. It is a cruel game for night to come and pretend the world should close her eyes and fall into dreams. Some of us can't dream, even when our eyes are closed. All I see is the predator, inching ever closer." – B. Thompson

The poetic description of sleeplessness hints at several of the struggles faced by sufferers who can't sleep:

- Feeling oppressed by sleeplessness
- Connection between insomnia and depression
- Thinking about sleep (and not sleeping) until it takes over waking time
- Self-medicating with drugs and alcohol to induce sleep

More than twenty-five years after suffering her first depressive episode, Rebecca Clayson has learned a few things about depression, and about herself. "Sufficient rest allows the mind to relax and sort through all the stimuli that occur in any given day. Too much can cause sluggishness; too little, frazzled nerves. A nap now and then can be really helpful. It seems to reset my brainwaves so I'm not overwhelmed by emotion or physically fatigued."

> "Getting enough sleep is critical for me. It is also one of my biggest challenges, both because I have young children and because I struggle with cyclical bouts of sleeplessness, which cause my depression. The strangest part about sleeplessness? It is when I am the most exhausted and in need of sleep that I can't fall asleep. It is like my body is fighting against itself, like a little child fighting against his parents to stay up just a little longer. I'd give anything to tell the child to give up the battle and enjoy the sleep." – Eva Greene*

The medical profession has argued for years that we need to get more sleep, 7-9 hours a night, on average. But why is sleep so important for our bodies and as a power tool against depression?

> "The answer to health is proper regeneration. That also means recognizing the body as an ever learning, adapting, renewing system of information. Without proper sleep and regeneration, the system will break down—and depressive symptoms appear." – Matt Edmund, M.D.

> "Sadly, my depression always sets in after nights without sleep. But thinking about sleep makes me worry about it more, and then I can't fall asleep. It is a vicious cycle. Sometimes I listen to meditations and practice breathing techniques in bed so I can calm down. But anytime I don't sleep, depression always follows." – R. Longmeyer

Indeed, a recent study showed that 87% of patients who were treated for insomnia experienced improvement to their mental health and less depression.

THE SCIENCE OF SLEEPING AND WAKING

The two primary hormones that impact sleep are melatonin and cortisol. Melatonin (which is produced in the pineal gland) is the hormone that triggers us to get tired and fall asleep, and cortisol (produced in the adrenal gland) is the hormone used to form glucose to induce the anti-stress and anti-inflammatory functions. Thus, any interference in either of these hormones and our bodily processes could prevent us from getting the rest we need.

> "After years of fighting against taking sleep medication, my doctor convinced me that not sleeping was worse for me than the medication. Now I at least know I have an option when the battle for the night begins." – Jodi Orgill Brown

Part of the process includes the circadian rhythm, which all plants and animals have built-in to their systems, referred to as the time-giver. The time-giver uses daylight as a signal and syncs with the brain's internal clock.

The body's connection to light stems from thousands of years of human adaptation to the Earth's normal cycles of the sun rising and setting. Light in the morning resets the circadian rhythm and tells the body it is time to be alert. Even dim light at night can prevent sleep, as it changes the body's natural melatonin levels, which signal the body that it is time to sleep.

Exposing your body to at least fifteen minutes but up to two hours of light signals the time-giver to wake up. Take advantage of the caffeine-like boost of light by setting lights on timers, or using multi-setting lamps to lighten gradually at specified times, preparing your body to wake up before your alarm even goes off.

THE ART OF SLEEPING AND WAKING

The benefit of sleep is that it restarts our systems, like restarting a computer, it wipes away all the open tabs of fatigue, worry and despair. It is a fresh start for our bodies and minds, repowering the batteries that keep us alert and alive.

That is not to say that all our problems will magically disappear when we wake, but certainly the intense moments should pass, and our minds will have the time to work on the problems we often cannot solve during the day.

For some, the mental challenge comes in arising after we wake. Feeling like a failure doesn't leave one anxious to get up and start a new day or a new time. What is important is giving yourself a reason to be up to ignite positive energy. Wake up with hope. But for many of us, waking up is as daunting as trying to fall asleep.

> "I need to know what I am doing the next day before I go to sleep. If I have no appointments or commitments, it is too easy to wake without purpose. And, if I don't have a reason to get up, I will stay in bed, waste the morning, feel guilty, and then trigger my depression." -- Tammy Warren

A group of Facebook users* who participate in a private depression forum made the following suggestions for how they get going in the morning:

- "I exercise the minute I can get out of bed and into some clothes. It starts my blood flowing and my heart beating."
- "Brew coffee. I inhale the smell and sip my first cup as I plan my day."
- "I get ready with my kids and volunteer at the school at the start of the day. Then we all have somewhere to go and I am not pushing them out, but joining alongside them as we go into the school."
- "Read the Bible."
- "All it takes is one splash of cold water on my face, and my mind and body start to wake up."
- "I crank up the music and get my body moving to the beat. It wakes me up, makes me happy, and kicks off my morning with some exercise."
- "Before I get out of bed, I roll over, grab my notebook, and write my priorities for the day. Then I know why I have to get out of bed."
- "I schedule client appointments in the morning so I have to be to work on-time and prepared."
- "Light! I need lots of bright light to wake up. If I don't want to

wake others, I use my phone screen."

- "My yoga and stretching routine begins before I even get out of bed. I start by stretching my legs, and then I edge them over the bedside and start to sit up. It gives me a little time to mentally prepare, and it helps me physically prepare to get up."

Sleeping and waking are critical but complex processes. If it were as easy as just letting go of stress or forming a routine, we'd all be sleeping like babies. In the meantime, read William Blake's poem, or better yet, memorize the words and recite them repeatedly until they calm you into slumber.

Little Heart Asleep

Sleep! sleep! beauty bright,
Dreaming o'er the joys of night;
Sleep! sleep! in thy sleep
Little sorrows sit and weep.

Sweet Babe, in thy face
Soft desires I can trace,
Secret joys and secret smiles,
Little pretty infant wiles.
As thy softest limbs I feel,
Smiles as of the morning steal
O'er thy cheek, and o'er thy breast
Where thy little heart does rest.

O! the cunning wiles that creep
In thy little heart asleep.
When thy little heart does wake
Then the dreadful lightnings break,

From thy cheek and from thy eye,
O'er the youthful harvests nigh.
Infant wiles and infant smiles
Heaven and Earth of peace beguiles.

by William Blake

PRESS ON.

Quick Sleeping Can-Do Tips:

- Avoid daytime napping.
- Establish a bedtime routine that prepares you to rest.
- Avoid eating, reading, watching TV, or performing similar activities in bed.
- Write in a notebook, journal, or app and record any thoughts on your mind that may keep you up thinking at night.
- Do not use a phone, computer, or electronic tablet within a hour of going to sleep.
- Meditate or do calming stretches to prepare your body for sleep.
- Pray.
- Don't eat within 1-2 hours of bedtime.
- Experiment with environmental conditions until you have an established sleep zone (temperature in the room, type of sheets, fullness of pillows, fabric of nightwear, proximity to others in the bed, bedroom, or house, etc.).
- Do deep breathing exercises to slow your heart rate and calm your body. (See the chapter on triggers for a variety of breathing exercises.)
- Go to bed fifteen minutes earlier than normal, then make earlier your nightly routine.

Quick Waking Can-Do Tips:

- Establish a regular wake-up time.
- Get out of bed when you're awake.
- Program your alarm or use an app to play upbeat or happy song.
- Begin the day with a morning mantra or positive affirmation.
- Get a light or clock that lights slowly and increases over the hour before you get up, preparing your body to wake.
- Create a commitment for yourself so you have to get out of bed (appointment, class, volunteer time, exercise, etc.).
- Establish morning traditions and routines that you enjoy.

- Put your alarm clock or phone in another room so you have to get out of bed to turn it off.
- When you get up, turn on lights to cue your body that it is time to wake. (Or, set timers to have bedroom lights go on with your alarm clock.)
- Do not vary your waking time by more than one hour, even on the weekends. Waking at the same time programs your body to rise. Don't throw yourself off with late nights or late mornings.

CHAPTER 14:
Self-Improvement Time

Feeling down in the dumps? Research has shown a powerful connection between mental health and learning at all stages in life. "Mental wellbeing means feeling good—about yourself and the world around you—and being able to get on with life in the way you want. Learning can boost self-confidence and self-esteem, help build a sense of purpose, and help us connect with others."[xii]

Camryn* never liked watching the news or current event stories. They were all so depressing and sad. She quit college to put her husband through school and never went back to finish her own degree. Once she had kids, her young children kept her busy, and she rarely had time to do things for herself. Her model-like figure sagged, and her once-adoring friends faded into the background.

She only went out to accompany her husband to work functions. Though she'd once been proud of being his trophy wife, she no longer felt like a trophy, and she didn't think she had anything to contribute to the conversations. She knew the latest Disney and Nickelodeon shows but didn't know all the world leaders or technology lingo. She hadn't heard of the trending gurus or the themes they spoke about. Every conversation and topic made her feel inadequate, behind the times, uneducated, or out of touch.

With every venture out into the world, she determined to socialize less, despite her growing needs to take a break from the kids and have some personal time. But Camryn felt stuck in a time warp; the world had moved forward ten years while she had changed diapers and colored with her kids.

This based-on-a-true-story scenario repeats itself in many forms. Whether it is a mother at home, a husband caught in a dead-end job, or an immigrant in a new land, thousands of us feel irrelevant, unheard, unseen or unloved. We *fall* into depression, tripped up, in part, because our self-evaluations *fall*. (Read tips for looking more truthfully at experiences in "Assigning Labels" in chapter four.)

How can we stop ourselves from falling into depression or into patterns of self-criticism? Philip Moeller in the Huffington Post said, "Your mind may be the closest thing to the Holy Grail of longevity and happiness. Education has been widely documented by researchers as the single variable tied most directly to improved health and longevity. *And when people are intensely engaged in doing and learning new things, their wellbeing and happiness can blossom.*"

When we are intensely absorbed in an activity, we lose track of place and time. Hours pass like minutes. Despite the effort exerted, we emerge energized and happy. (This condition is known as "flow," a name coined thirty years ago by psychologist Mihaly Csikszentmihalyi.)

- "When I am depressed, minutes take hours. But when I am learning something new, or practicing something I am trying to master, the reverse is true. I study endlessly about topics many people have never even heard of. But I rock at Trivial Pursuit. It is not useless trivia to me, it is priceless, because learning keeps me going." – Brandon T. Orgill

Harvard professor Lisa Berkman says, "Your mind is really like a muscle and mental wellbeing, including happiness, and using it is a key."

"I go to a weekly Bible study class. For me, it is not just about religion, it is also about understanding the time periods and peoples I read about. I learn about cultures and languages and I realize how much I don't know. Going to class gives me mental stimulation, and it helps me be more social than I would be on my own." – E. B.

Learned skills (even skills that you might categorize as brain functions more than skills) add to competency levels and increase the likelihood that you will have, and feel, the ability to contribute.

Take, for example, learning a new language. Even without the use of medical technology such as x-rays and MRI scans to analyze brain function, anyone who engages in learning a new language realizes that practical skills are gained from the experience. These include: heightened conversational abilities, a greater mastery of languages in general (including the learner's native language), better study skills, greater discipline, and enhanced concentration and focus.

When you engage your mental faculties in a task, whether it be reading (or listening to) a book, practicing an instrument, playing a sport or learning a game, the brain switches from self-focusing to engagement in the new activity. You cannot multitask your brain to the point where you are thinking about your depressive pit and practicing a new language at the same time. While you may be able to walk and talk, that's because the walking part does not require active cognitive faculties, as most people have mastered walking. You don't have to think about it. But when learning something new, the brain must actively participate in the process. When your brain is engaged, your other thoughts will drop off your worry list and your happy hormones increase so you rise above a depressed state.

> "I cannot testify about the benefits of learning so much as I can testify about the negative consequences of being mentally dormant. After I graduated from high school, I wanted to be forever finished with school and learning. But the longer I plugged away at no to low-skill jobs, the more depressed I became. I made no progress and had no goals. I took little from the world and added nothing. I wasn't just purposeless, I was truly lost." – J.T.

But it is not just classroom education that kicks the brain into action. Whether you study interior design, computer programming, or you pick up woodcarving, the practice can benefit your wellbeing.

Practical skills often equate to increased self-confidence, which create a dopamine boost in the learner. It gives you a little reward for your hard work.

But trying new things can be scary.

Many of us cringe at the thought of trying something new. Why?

Most often we fear: 1) the unknown; 2) the possibility of failure; 3) embarrassing ourselves; or 4) physical harm.

Yet, flexing our mental muscles provides neuropsychological benefits and psychological/emotional health benefits, as well, says Dr. Stephanie Smith. Benefits include:

1. **Stress Relief.** Why? When we break out of normal routines, we have to think more consciously about our activities, and therefore think less about our worries.

2. **Play.** Learning a new skill can incorporate fun back into life. Research has shown that time spent playing rejuvenates the mind and contributes to happiness. So pick up a new skill to get your heart pounding with joy again. Not sure what to try? Think of an activity, sport, or skill you enjoyed or wanted to develop as a child (skiing, cooking, running, archery, writing, swimming) and dive in.

3. **Sociality.** Social bonds are formed through shared experiences. What better way to beef up your social life than to pick up a hobby and meet new people?

4. **Structure.** School and organized classroom learning provides built-in goals, defined steps, and progress markers. This structure makes it easier to accomplish goals and *feel* accomplished. And, process is key for not only abstract thinkers but also those who suffer from severe clinical depression and other mental health disorders, who may struggle with achieving goals because they lack the skills to break them down into manageable steps that will take them from points A to E.

5. **Perspective.** Learning provides background from which you can view the world. When you gain knowledge, you broaden your understanding of people, cultures, times and events.

Whether you learn for the chance to contribute or contribute through the things you've learned, you will find your place in the world grows along with your knowledge and skills.

PRESS ON.

Quick Self-Improvement Can-Do Tips:

- Read a nonfiction, self-help, or historical fiction book.
- Listen to a podcast (you can find podcasts on any topic, hobby, interest or business subject, so pick an interest, then pick a podcast).
- Learn a new game.
- Take a history class.
- Take on a new responsibility at work, such as learning to use an IT system or understanding the monthly reports.
- Listen to an audio book (better yet, listen while you walk).
- Watch or listen to a TED talk.
- Learn a language—Use Duolingo or other language learning apps for fun practice.
- Play a brain game (Sudoku, Chess, Scrabble, Settlers of Catan, Monopoly, Lexogon, Boggle, Sequence, Word on the Street, Bananagrams; Electronic games: Quiz Up, Word Scramble, Geometry Wars, Words with Friends, Spell Tower, Letter Press, Type Shift)
- Read a religious text.
- Try the latest fitness craze at your local gym.
- Learn to cook a favorite restaurant dish that you've never tried to make at home.
- Visit a gallery or museum and learn about a person or period in history that interests you.
- Fix that broken bike or garden gate. Once you've done that, how about setting yourself a bigger DIY project? There are lots of free video tutorials online.
- Sign up for a course for a practical skill, such as plumbing or gardening.
- Rediscover an old hobby that challenges you, whether it's making model airplanes, writing stories, refinishing furniture, or sewing.

CHAPTER 15:
Nature

We exist in a world where humans hold immense power, and yet possess little control.

Nowhere is this more evident than in nature. When we step outside, we see how small we are in relation to the universe. But still, this very Earth, whose magnitude could engulf us, also affirms our presence and gives us peace—because we are part of her.

"To embrace nature is to embrace your place in it."
– Jessica Thornton

Before we lived in high-rise buildings, with sewage systems and electricity. We were children of the land. Today, when people fall into bouts of depression, solace can often be found in nature once again.

"The more time I spend in nature, the more I am convinced that the great outdoors is a depression buster." – Jodi Orgill Brown

It is comforting to know no matter how low you feel, the moon and the stars sit in the heavens every night. The night sky is not unchanging, yet it is constant, and there is solace to be held in that promise.

"Nature can be renewing to the soul; the colors, the scents, the peace and quiet, fresh air, warmth from the sun, the gentle sound of rain, all help restore emotional balance." – Rebecca Clayson

People turn to nature for the same reasons people turn to books or television: a sense of catharsis or escapism, a sense of belonging or adventure. But nature is more than a distraction from life, nature is the essence of life. Nature is the process of living, growing, decaying, dying, and giving back to life, as seen in a million scenarios just outside our doors.

The Inspiration of Nature
by Jessica Thornton

Nature has always been the subject of human fascination. The beauty and wonder of nature has inspired people to create for centuries. Water lilies inspired Monet and the night sky inspired Van Gogh. Walt Whitman's *Song of Myself* explores the relationship between humans and the environment. Nature, and finding our place within it, motivates people to live, move, investigate, map, and create, all of which engage the mind and soul and block negativity.

Carl Sagan once said, "If you wish to make apple pie from scratch, you must first create the universe." By that, he meant whatever you wish to make today is ultimately the byproduct of years and years of creation within the universe. Before you could have an apple or piecrusts or flour or eggs, you needed the birth of the cosmos, galaxies, and our own sun.

It stands to reason that your very existence is only possible because of everything that came before you. The universe, and all that exists within it, was made to be experienced by you. Even at your lowest points, the entirety of the natural world waits for you.

Nature's Antidepressants

Nature lifts the spirit and engages us with the world.

Sunlight is a proven antidepressant. "Natural sunlight is much brighter than indoor lighting, over a hundred times brighter, on average. Even the natural light of a gray, cloudy day is several times brighter than the inside of most people's houses."[xiii] More than a hundred studies prove the therapeutic effects of being outside, including the healing effects of light and vitamin D.

In fact, going outside provides a better boost and more happiness than getting a raise at work. Nature, more than money or things, assuages depression. When you are feeling down, step outside.

> "After surgery it struck me that I needed to get outside. From that moment on, my daughter and I were always outside. I started walking a mile or more a day to be out in the sunshine. Never again was I going to be confined to a house that I had no say in. The more time we spent outside exercising, the fewer my symptoms. Getting outside in the sunshine and exercising topped off the healing." — Brandi Nicole Astle

Even in winter, studies have proven the benefits of getting outside, for as few as five minutes a day. Bundle up, put on your scarf, and head out. A quick walk around the block with the dog can do wonders for your mood and your spirit.

> "Being outside, even for ten minutes at a time, totally changes me. Something about not being in confined spaces, perhaps just the openness, gives me perspective. And I need the natural light to feel healthy and happy.
>
> As I've gotten older, I've learned to recognize the beauty of things outside: trees, grass, flowers, clouds, and sunsets. I realize how amazing it all is. I intentionally take breaks throughout the day to go sit on the porch for a few minutes and soak it in. No matter what other commitments I have, if I take breaks outside, then I can go back inside and keep going. Then I'll do again a few hours later. Going out, into nature, becomes a ritual in my day.
>
> I also like to work outside, even pulling weeds, mowing the lawn, or shoveling in the snow in the winter. When it snows, it gets me out there, gets me moving, and gives me the benefits of being outside. Then I'm active, I shovel, I move, I'm out there, and I come in ready for a cup of hot chocolate. There is something therapeutic about it.
>
> My neighbors joke that they always see me outside, and I tell them, 'Be worried if you don't see me outside. That is when I am bad; that is when I am not remembering that I need to get out.'
>
> Nature is a reset. Need a lift? Go outside and reset." — Tami O. Baker

Nature's other antidepressants include growing plants, flowers, and gardens. Set a pot outside on your steps, veranda, or deck and watch your happiness grow. The time and engagement with nature, for even a few minutes, creates happiness and connection. And gardening is a great way to try some new herbs or vegetables and get a little green going in your life.

Natural Perspective

Even in the devastation caused by natural events, we cannot help but see the power of Mother Nature. Only humans deem natural occurrences as disasters—on a larger scale, they are just part of a changing world. Perspective reminds us that though we may get in the way of nature, she does not get in our way. In the same vein, the explorer/philosopher Alfred Wainwright wrote, "There is no such thing as bad weather, only unsuitable clothing." Sometimes we need to be reminded that control comes in our response to circumstances we have no control of.

The world is much larger than a pocket-sized screen or the inside walls of a bedroom. When we get out of a place where we are trapped in our minds, our thoughts immediately change our perspective and frame of reference. When we see that we are part of something much grander than being simply individuals, or even part of one family, or one relationship, we begin to see our part in the symphony of life. The birds whistle their tunes, the wind chimes in with the woodwind sounds of the breeze, waves laps against the shores of a lake, water trickles, splashes, or crashes down a stream or waterfall, even the bugs buzz in perfect harmony with nature. Listening, observing, and stepping into your role in it all is a humbling and empowering experience.

"Few experiences rank higher on my Top Ten life list than moments spent in nature. But it is not triumphing over nature that leads to a sense of personal satisfaction, rather that I am a part of nature, a small part of a big, beautiful equation.

Recently, my family enjoyed the scenery around Zion's National Park, one of the country's most geographically diverse areas. We planned a series of hikes that would lead us through slot canyons, traversing rivers and summiting one of the nation's most incredible peaks. The moment we stepped foot on the first trail, the sense of adventure zinged through me.

At our initial river crossing, we carefully planned our steps to cross without getting wet. We jumped, hopped, and tried to balance on unsteady river rocks. We finished the first mile with little more than a few splashes of water on our bodies. In the beginning, that was part of the fun. As the hike continued, we crisscrossed the river numerous times, taking pride in who could stay dry along the way. Our methods grew in creativity and we used logs, rocks, and our best parkour movements to bound or tiptoe over the rushing water.

Eventually, the path stopped crossing the streams and took us directly into the river. The snowmelt water swamped my shoes, and immediately I became part of the river. The game changed from staying dry to getting soaked. We entered the slot canyon, surrounded by towering red rock walls reaching to the sky. The elevation increased with every step forward, and we came to a waterfall. We climbed the rocks through the cascading stream until we reached the swirling, sparkling pool at the top. The cold, the fear, and the games disappeared. We were simply part of the earth and her grand design.

By the time we returned to our car, parked at the trailhead several miles back, I felt total peace and joy. Cold toes, wet clothes, and muddy shoes could not dampen my at-one-ness with nature. For the first time in many weeks, my body and mind were not consumed by my own sensations and thoughts, but by the sheer exhilaration and perfection of the surroundings—and my place in them." – Jodi Orgill Brown

Early Native American Indian tribes are known for their peaceful relationships with nature, their love of the land and of all things from the earth. Their respect extends to every object and living thing on the planet. Early tribal people had little sense of anything outside of nature. Even their own names reflected Mother Earth and her inhabitants. Perhaps when we come to appreciate nature, we find peace within her limitless boundaries.

Even the smallest element in nature teaches us lessons and gives us perspective. Consider the principles we learn from:

- Waves which travel thousands of miles across the planet, rolling, thundering, and finally plummeting against the shore.
- Cacti that grow in the desert.
- Flowers that take root in the cracks between rocks.
- Weeds that stretch hundreds of feet beneath the surface,

persistent until they find a small space to push upward and emerge from below.

- Millions of living creatures, in the seas, skies, and earth, which most men never see, but which contribute to our ecosystem.
- Individual drops of water, which erode great mountains and smooth sharp rocks into polished gems.
- Natural camouflage abilities of plants and animals.
- Great forests of trees that grow together, protect each other, and reach ever higher toward the sun.
- The water cycle.
- Rain, which provides life-giving water to all creatures.
- Wild berries and plants that provide rich color, beauty, and nutrients to living creatures.
- Poisons that are used to create cures.
- Rivers that carry sediment across the globe.
- Trees and plants that naturally create oxygen, which we need to live.
- Weeds that flower and create colorful beauty in the landscape.
- Clouds that travel the skies and mingle with the sun to paint the heavens.

Perspective, like experience, can change our thoughts and elevate us to a higher plane.

NATURAL ENGAGEMENT

Put a child in nature and they can entertain themselves for hours. A tiny shovel, a plot of dirt, a sandbox, or a trickle of water is all it takes for little minds and bodies to be fully captured by the miracles of Mother Nature's everyday devices. Many elementary school children experience the awe and joy of planting a miniature seed in a paper cup and dutifully watering and sunning the dirt until a green seedling pushes its way through the barriers and into the light. Nature engages our minds and bodies and shows us that living things change and grow.

Consider the difference between a drive and a ride. When you drive in the car, you can see nature, but from a limited perspective.

127

However, if you ride a bike or motorcycle the same distance, you are absorbed by nature, you don't simply view it.

Engagement is more rigorous than involvement; engagement is captivation with an activity, a state that does not allow our brains to split focus, making it impossible to think about depression.

Nature is the ultimate natural upper.

PRESS ON.

Quick Nature Can-Do Tips:

- Have breakfast or lunch outside on a porch, deck, or even on the bench or steps outside your apartment or office.
- Walk to work, school, the grocery store, or just plan a few minutes a day dedicated to being outside and in nature. Try not to fill the time with phone calls, music, or texts, just be part of it and enjoy.
- Find an oasis near your home, school, or office. Even a shady spot under a tree, a bench, a bridge, a picnic table, swing, flower garden, or dock can provide needed comfort and uplift when made part of your routine. Visit it often and make it special to you.
- Take a pet for a walk. Imagine nature from your pet's eyes.
- Take your laptop outside to work.
- Ride a bike. Cycling is a great way to accomplish multiple goals at once, from being in nature to exercising to eating healthy (you can't buy large quantities of soda or alcohol if you are carting it home on a bike).
- Combine nature with a hike in the mountains or walk in the park, and you've got exercise covered, too.
- Watch a rainstorm, or better yet, go outside and dance in the rain
- Open the blinds so you can observe life around you
- Grab your phone and take pictures of your favorite places in nature. Keep the photos on as your screensaver or home screen so you always have a personal reminder.
- Take photos of the landscapes of your home, as a reminder that you have a place that beckons you and where you belong.
- Open the windows and listen to the sounds of nature. Try to identify individual noises that accent your environment
- Grow something! Even a small seed in a paper cup can provide a boost. If possible, plant a favorite flower or herb so you can bring the best of nature indoors.
- Plant a garden.
- Visit a nearby park and play in a stream or lake.

- Build a sandcastle (at a beach or in a sandbox).
- Download apps and listen to nature sounds when you wake or before you fall asleep. Some of our favorites:
    1. Relax Melodies: Sleep Sounds by iLBSoft
    2. Nature Melody: Soothing, Calming, and Relaxing Sounds by Lina Elsayed
    3. Alarm Clock: Sleep Sounds Pro by iLBSoft
    4. Insight Timer by Insight Network

CHAPTER 16:
Creativity

Whether art reflects life, or life reflects art may be less important than knowing that art *heals* life. Creating outward expressions from inner thoughts and feelings releases our emotions, and restores our souls.

THE CREATIVE RELEASE
by Jessica Thornton

Creativity is the ultimate showcase of the human spirit. Creativity is what took humans to the moon, what gave us life-saving vaccinations, what designed the tablet you may or may not be reading this on. Creativity is the lovechild of curiosity and innovation, birthed from our inwardly expansive minds.

When you think of expressing yourself creatively, art is what probably comes to mind first. And while painting and drawing definitely lend themselves to creative expression, creativity manifests itself in almost all walks of life. Coding a computer program or creating a video game requires creativity. Reading a book and imagining the characters and worlds in your own mind require creativity. Exercise can be creative in the sheer number of ways you can be good to your body.

Ultimately, though, what all creativity has in common is the ability to heal and relieve. Writing, reading, sculpting, carving, painting, drawing, building, photography, videography, and gardening—the options are limitless. It stimulates positive brain waves because it is fulfilling and fun. The act of creating something, whatever it may be, is uplifting. Your creation may have been dreamt from your own mind, or maybe you collaborated with someone to produce something meaningful, useful, or beautiful to the both of you. There are worlds within you, waiting to be explored. Your method of tapping into those worlds will require some creativity and, hopefully, uplift you.

The power of creativity extends beyond the process itself. We can receive the same feelings of happiness (from a release of serotonin in the body) from enjoying creations from others or reviewing our own creative triumphs. When you need a boost, look at or read something you've created and let the joy flow.

> "I love beautiful things that others have created. It thrills my soul, probably in the way a day at Disneyland excites some people. For me, happiness comes from seeing brush strokes, color, and creative connections in ordinary life. The way the wires on the telephone poles come together or seeing beauty in nature, I am inspired by creations and art that are all around us." – Kathy Wade

Kathy's struggle with depression started as a young child, and she has spent years intentionally searching for tools to cope. She works tirelessly to surround herself by creations that spark her mind and thrill her soul. Kathy strives to design her environment, but has also trained herself to see the beauty in every day things.

CREATIVITY AND COLOR
by Rebecca Clayson

It has long been known that color affects mood. Advertisers use color to their advantage; some colors stimulate while others pacify. Blue, a color with longer wavelengths, has been known to have a calming effect on the brain, while red, with shorter wavelengths, has an opposite effect.

In Huffpost Healthy Living, Rachel Grumman Bender states, "If you think of the way we describe certain emotions (seeing red, feeling blue, green with envy), there's no denying that color and mood are inextricably linked." Although reaction to color is subjective and affected by cultural norms, it is safe to say that vibrant colors produce energy while blander hues have a calming effect.

132

Knowing this information can be helpful in a number of ways. It can impact your emotions when creating something artistically. Maybe you'll see the things you are feeling reflected in art you are creating or consuming. You could also use this information to create a healthy atmosphere for yourself within your home. If you find a color that particularly resonates with you or makes you feel at peace, you can paint your bedroom that color, or decorate parts of your home with those colors. You can integrate those colors into your clothes.

ART AND THERAPY

"Art makes sense. It speaks to me."
-- Kathy Wade

Using the senses to explore how we feel empowers us to take control of our out-of-control or overpowering thoughts. Connecting with emotions and expressing them artistically is therapeutic; it gets the overwhelm out of us and into our art form.

The effects are so powerful, they are practiced in therapies throughout the world, and in 1969, the American Art Therapy Association was established to help creativity heal people.

Trained art therapist Routa Segal says, "Creative art therapy is a journey of finding out who you are, where you are, what you have, and what you need to get you where you want to be in life."

Enjoying art has curative benefits, as well. From storytelling to drama to sculpture to painting, art is about expression—of emotions, ideas, concerns, triumphs, frustrations, joys, and disappointments. The thoughts that we can't let go of mentally need to come out some how. Art releases thoughts from our minds and captures them in the way that feels right to our souls.

THE POWER OF CREATION

"Create something that will contribute a tiny fleck to the universe."
– Brandon T. Orgill

For many people with depression, creativity has become an outlet for them to find relief. Both creating something new, or taking the old and making it new, bring feelings of satisfaction.

"I like to see something worn out or old and make it beautiful again. I buy old furniture and refinish it or paint it. And I like the thought of doing the same things within ourselves.

As a mother of five and a foster mother, personal time is limited, but creative time is a must. I don't often get the chance to sit down and be creative just for the sake of it, so I make it a priority by doing art with my kids. I love to see them with paint brushes in hand, excited to create something." — Kathy Wade

Jodi Orgill Brown says, "I love to create, but I am not very artistic. But if something speaks beauty to me, I enjoy it every time I see it, even if it is full of imperfections. Thus, my novice attempts at painting, wood whittling, or drawing make me happy both during the creation process and every time I see the results. It takes me out of any hard realities I may be facing and thrusts me into a time warp of creation."

The *process* of creation heals the mind, as much or more than the artistic outcome.

"When I was teaching art classes to kids in my neighborhood one summer, my family was hit by a major life challenge. Things had been particularly hectic and I'd been stressed and depressed, but those classes turned into such a blessing because my home was full of kids who were excited to paint and do art!

"But more than that, I was constantly thinking about what to teach and how to teach it in unique, fun, inspiring ways. My brain was in creative mode NONSTOP and it felt so good! I did not search the Internet for ideas; I worked my own brain and did my own thinking. That was a MAJOR antidepressant for me. My brain was constantly spinning and churning, and the ideas kept coming and coming. I didn't even have to actually create anything to feel that thrill; even just thinking about it had an amazing effect on my mood." — Kathy Wade

THE CREATIVE CONNECTION

Creativity boosts come in any endeavor in which we choose to solve a problem or do something in a different way than we've done before.

> "Even little things, like finding a new way to organize my house or cook a beautiful meal for my family, make me happy. I find joy in rearranging a room or finding new ways to help my kids learn to spell. It sounds silly, but creativity sparks happiness for me. It doesn't matter as much what I do, as long as I do something in a new way." — Kathy Wade

If depression has made your mind and perceptions a chaotic place, channeling your focus or energy into creating something, is a means of fighting that chaos, which is a triumph within itself.

THE GOAL OF CREATIVITY

By Brandon T. Orgill

If you've read this chapter and thought it cannot be of service to you because you do not think of yourself as a creative person, fear not. Everyone is a creator. All of our brains are wired for creative problem solving, brainstorming, and different forms of creativity. Even if there's one "type" of creativity that you don't connect with, there will be one that you do connect with.

I would argue before any other purposes, creating something should first and foremost be fulfilling for the creator.

By creating, we progress and the world becomes better and brighter, something that might have become nothing now becomes something, and happiness flourishes. Creation of a better you, of a poem, of a house, of a business, of art -- it doesn't matter what you create. It simply matters that you do create.

Progression is the goal and creation is a vehicle to get you there.
(Read the full essay by Brandon in Part III.)

PRESS ON.

Quick Creation Can-Do Tips

- Freewrite or brainstorm. Writ nonstop for a limited amount. Re-read to find themes or ideas you can further explore creatively.

- Start doodling whatever comes to mind or whatever you see.

- Take a class of an art, craft, or skill you are interested in pursuing or learning more about. You're never too old to try something new and you're never too experienced to have nothing new to learn.

- Don't have any supplies? Just grab a pen and write your name in your own version of calligraphy. Or write a few sentences and design your own personal font.

- Watch an online art tutorial and try it on the spot. Think of your favorite animal, car, or cartoon character and learn instantly how to bring it to life on a page.

- Make a new food. Just open your cupboard and fridge, see what you have and Google "recipes" with the list of your ingredients.

- Make a favorite food in a new way. Experiment and see what happens. No ideas? Make a peanut butter and jam sandwich, butter it, and then grill it liked a grilled cheese sandwich. Voila, a whole new experience from an old idea.

- Revisit an old hobby, something you maybe abandoned long ago because you just got too busy to keep at it. Try something you used to love and see how it feels now.

- Build a world. Think of your ideal environment (mountains, beach, nature with no bugs) and imagine what your perfect world would look like.

- If all else fails, tear out this page of your book and turn it into a paper airplane. Google it and see how many unique ways you can make your page can fly.

CHAPTER 17:

Sociality

For thousands of years, human survival and progress depended on giving and receiving help from others. Hunting, traveling, herding, farming, and family security all required multiple individuals doing their parts to help the whole.

The Native American Indian tribe, the Anasazi, called this "The Path of We". Each person came together for the benefit of all. There was no differentiation between the hunter, whose arrow pierced the animal, or those who carried the animal back to the tribe, or the animal whose sacrifice allowed for families to eat. All contributions were accepted equally.

"Would it surprise you to hear that man's unhappiness is due in large measure to the way he is seeking after happiness?

You already know this from your own life. For when you have been unhappy, you have been unhappy with others — with your father or mother, your sister or brother, your spouse, your son, your daughter.

If unhappiness is with others, wouldn't it stand To reason that happiness must be with others as well?"

-- *The Seven Paths*, by the Anasazi Foundation

Today, technology and industry have made it seem like we don't need other. But the opposite is still true. In fact, technology, which limits face-to-face interaction, has created a whole new series of problems that didn't exist years ago. We may be able to order take-out food, clothes, groceries, and entertainment with the touch of a screen, but we are missing out on human touch and contact. The effect of less human contact is that people feel more alone, which evokes alone time and trigger fears of interacting with others.

Teens often face a double-edged sword: they are part of a group, but that membership can be revoked at any time, leaving them isolated and alone. Junior high and high schools can be torture chambers for those who are on the fringe, those who have been kicked out of their tribe, and for those who simply never fit in to begin with. Even seemingly insignificant details or situations (wearing the "wrong" clothes or living in the "wrong" neighbor-hood), can make a young person victim of shaming, out-casting them from participation in social groups. Yet, sociality is critical to establish healthy relationships and so teens feel they belong—and have someone who cares.

THE ADDICTION DISCONNECTION

What happens to those who don't establish healthy relationships? "When we're happy and healthy, we bond with each other. But if you can't do that, because you are traumatized, isolated, or beaten down by life, you will bond with something that will give you relief. That might be gambling, pornography, cocaine, or cannabis, but you will bond with something...because that is our nature as human beings," says researcher, Johann Hari. "Evidence suggests addiction is about not being able to bear to be present in your life."[xiv]

Addiction is a sad, but preventable next-step for many depressives. When the isolation of depression becomes unbearable, we reach for something to make it bearable, some-thing, because we often can't face someone.

Isolation may be self-imposed to help us avoid reminders of what we don't have in our lives.

Depressives and addicts are starving for bonds.

CRAVING SOCIALITY

The effect of social bonds can often be seen when a depressive (or addict) is thrust into a social situation.

Nathan Ogden didn't understand or experience depression until he broke his neck and became a quadriplegic from a ski accident.

"As much as it sucks to go out and socialize when I'm depressed, 90% of the time I am glad I did. I truly believe if you keep saying no then it becomes easier and easier to stay inside. Then that depression and darkness grow bigger and bigger until the light is so dim it's nearly impossible to see." -- Nathan Ogden (Read his essay in Part III.)

Researcher and author, Stephen Ilardi writes, "The research on this issue is clear: When it comes to depression, relationships matter. People who lack a supportive social network face an increased risk of becoming depressed, and of remaining depressed once an episode strikes."

Social support reduces the influence of stress and fosters a sense of meaning and purpose in life. In addition, emotional support from social ties enhances psychological wellbeing, which, in turn, may reduce the risk of unhealthy behaviors and poor physical health.

SAFETY NET

"Personal relationships form a safety net around individuals to protect them from too much isolation."[xv]

Often when you are alone, you feel alone, which isn't healthy for anyone. "Socializing helps me, in fact, it is in my daily toolbox of self care, because frankly, I deteriorate rapidly if I don't talk to people outside of work in a 24-hour period," says author and sufferer, Dyany Munson.

"When I am feeling depressed the only way I am able to break out of it is to force myself to be social or go see the family I claim. If for nothing else than to remind myself why I am still around and things can and will get better. Nothing relieves the feelings more than getting hugged by my nieces and nephews and just remembering that life can be fun. I struggled with depression and suicidal thoughts most of my adolescent life and the only reason I got through it was forcing myself to be with friends. Good people in your life can help you overcome anything." -- Chris Finch

Sufferer M. K.* learned to recognize her triggers so she knew when it was critical to be social. "I had to teach myself and get myself out of my comfort zone. I still have days where I don't want to leave the house, talk to anyone or even get out of bed but I have to force myself to do it, being social even if its just going to the store and making eye contact and smiling at someone is enough."

THE RIGHT DOSE

But every situation and individual is unique, so persons must first know their normal socialization levels, before making changes or forcing interactions during depression.

> "You first need to know your ideal baseline for sociality. Since I am autistic, frequent socializing leads to higher anxiety and worse depression, and everybody will have a different baseline and different specific social needs (enjoying crowds, being with family, large groups versus intimate groups, etc.). After that is accounted for, put me in the group of those who do better when they push themselves to stay close to their ideal." -- Kara Forsyth Cottle

The right level of sociality depends on the person and the situation.

> "If it is people that know me well it usually helps me quite a bit to force myself to be social. Those they are closest to me can tell when I'm trying to 'fake it till I make it,' and call me out on it. Those are also the people I feel comfortable talking with. In those situations I am glad I force myself to go and be social.
>
> When it is people I am not close to or don't know at all it usually makes the depression worse. It just wears me out to slap on a smile and pretend nothing is wrong." -- Rachel Decker Bolin

Spending time with the right people, those who are supportive of your efforts, is also key when depression grabs hold.

> "Being social is difficult when my depression is at its worst. I'm very good at putting up a face and pretending that everything is ok. When I do get the courage to go out and be social, it does help. One important factor for me is whom I am being social with. Some people can make it worse, others make me forget for a moment. When I'm at my lowest, I try to only spend time with the people that I know lift me up." -- Randi Spicer

Sufferers without emotional support must find ways to create a support system to press on.

> "As much as we sometimes hate the thought of being with other people,

we can't live without them. I've had Bell's Palsy since I was eight years old. I've not had much help and emotional support. Not many hugs, not much sympathy, not much care.

But to fight it, I figured it out myself.

The dark thoughts will go if I go out.

My uncle once told my mom to lock me at home because the way I look was humiliating (for him). This is patched on my memory. But then I swore, 'I'll never lock myself inside! I'll travel,' I promised myself, 'I'll go to University in another town, I'll work in another town, I'll travel as much as I possibly can.'

I'm still depressed from time to time, but I know that locking myself in my room never does anything good to me." -- Fika Mariana

Anytime depression is compounded or complicated by serious life issues, the need and level of sociality can change.

"Being in the grieving stages from losing my daughter, as well as post-partum, I feel like I have hit the jackpot on depression. There are so many days where I don't want to be social or even answer the phone, and those are the days I know I need to be social most. I don't go out to the park or in the midst of civilization but I do visit one friend. I let my kids play while I visit. I am lucky enough that my friends are very understanding—if I am quiet and at a breaking point, they can lead the conversation and not feel awkward.

Normally, I do feel better once I have gone home after visiting with friends, not only for me but for my kids. I also have the outlet of working out to release the endorphins to help me get out of the 'funk'.

If you have a close friend you can visit to be 'sociable' that understands, then it's not as hard because you don't feel like a burden.

Of course there are the days where the only thing that seems to do the job is good ol' Netflix." -- Sadee Carney

Young mother, Kendra Miller, has learned that being around the wrong people makes depression worse. Her tactic is to avoid individuals with whom she has a history of emotional struggles. However, she acknowledges the benefits of being around people, even if you aren't social with them.

"Being social only helps me if I can be with someone I love having around, then it helps my depression immensely. But, running errands, where I don't have to talk to anyone, but do get out of the house [and around people], also helps me a lot." -- Kendra Miller

"Target is my best friend when I can't face the prospect of another Friday night alone. I can't stay home and rearrange my shoes one more time, but somehow getting out, even just walking around the store, helps me avoid a depressive funk. I feel positive energy from other people, even if I don't say a word." -- H.C.

Part of the Team

The need for acceptance is so strong, some people will do just about anything to belong to a group that gives them identity and connection. They will join gangs or start unhealthy habits, such as drinking or smoking, just to fit in.

In the movie, *Courageous*, a police officer must arrest a young man he knows because of gang activity. The officer questions the young man, pleading to know why he was involved with the gang. The teen boy cries in response, "I ain't got nobody. I just ain't got nobody." As simple as that, he turned toward a group who would accept him and make him feel like he had somebody, even when it meant putting his life on the line.

Belonging to a group creates identity. Leaving a group, either naturally or because you are forced out, can feel like an identity crisis. U.S. Veteran, Phil Ritzert, experienced this after finishing his military service.

"I can only explain depression from my point of view, which is from a Veteran's standpoint. The reason I say that is because I never experienced anything like depression prior to leaving the military after four separate deployments to Iraq.

Once the military and war were no longer the major driving force in my life I became lost, and depressed for a long time. Some of that depression obviously had direct ties to PTSD, but I think a lot of it was feeling like I walked away from the only thing I was ever good at, which was soldiering. That was a major problem for me, society says killing and hating are not good things, so I had a very poor self-image in the civilian world. In the military I was often referred to as a mercenary, I volunteered for all four combat tours. I was good at war so I was borderline worshipped for surviving so much time in combat. In the military I was hailed for the things society said were undesirable, so leaving that environment took a huge toll on me. Here's why I think that's important. Once I was a civilian, I assumed other civilians should dislike me because I strayed from society's moral code of right and wrong, albeit while at war. I withdrew, from family, friends, society, everything and everyone. The more I withdrew, the more depressed I got.

When I finally sought help, and began putting my life back together, a large part of that was reintegrating into social environments. Becoming part of a group again. Over the years I've had setbacks, and fell back into depressive states, and I've learned something very valuable: without regular, healthy social interactions I can become quite self-destructive. Staying happy now means being social, at least for me." -- Phil Ritzert

The strength from feeling accepted is a powerful motivator. Unfortunately, desiring social acceptance can spur us to give up values, in exchange for approval.

"You live in the age of the 'I,
And the age is taking its toll.

Modern man looks out for himself and
only secondarily for others. He is consumed with
satisfying his own personal 'needs.'

Ironically, man's obsession with personal
wants has obscured his greatest need—
the need to live in harmony with others."

-- *The Seven Paths*, by the Anasazi Foundation

Sometimes we don't reach out or socialize with others because of how depression makes us feel. Broken. Inadequate. Defective.

Erika Krull, MSEd, LMHP, has spent years helping people understand depression, and giving them tools to help keep going. "Depression is a selfish, abusive captor. It enjoys nothing more than seeing you all alone, feeling like nobody would miss you if you weren't around. It magnifies your sense of shame, making sure you believe that no one could understand or care about your struggles."

"Being social when I'm in my depression is difficult. I tend to want to be alone. I always feel like I have two options if I choose to be social:

1) Go and bring everybody down, making them miserable.
2) Go and pretend like I'm okay, put on a show, then slip gratefully into bed when I'm finally home.

I don't like pretending. Sometimes that's what it takes. While there, it feels like isolation in the middle of a crowd. Like everybody's there but nobody really sees the true me hiding behind the face." -- Julianne Kelsch

FINDING A SAFE PLACE

Part of life is having I-don't-want-to-be-in-this-place moments, but having an ally can change a battle — or a life.

"I have suffered from depression all my adult life and there's been so many times that I didn't want to be social (which is so against my nature because I truly love people and I often say talking is one of my favorite hobbies). When I'm so depressed that I can't concentrate or even have the desire to talk, it depresses me even more. I've learned through the years if I push myself to just try to be social it ends up being just what I needed to feel better. It's through being social and talking to others that not only have I've been helped, but I often feel I was able to help someone else." -- Alesia Budd

We all need a safe place to cry for help. Knowing you always have someone to lean on makes the hard days more manageable. If you don't have a good support system or a trusted friend with a listening ear, start looking at those around you. Who do you click with? Is there anyone you'd like to spend more time with, or be more like? Reach out to start a conversation or lend a helping hand. Even the beginnings of a new friendship serve a purpose.

"If you have a few people in your life who are genuinely concerned for your wellbeing, then hold on to them. They are a priceless part of your life and depression recovery. However, if you have toxic, unreliable individuals in your life, be very careful. These people may use your personal vulnerability to their advantage, hurting you time and again. A pastor or mental health counselor may be a good place to start if this is your situation.

Social support goes way beyond your friends trying to cheer you up a little. It's about making genuine connections and spending time with people who care about you. It's about knowing that you matter to other people. Depression can create a pit of despair and hopelessness inside you. With your loved ones nearby, the pit won't be nearly as frightening. Your safety net is ready to keep you from falling in.

The good times mean even more when you've been through some valleys together." -- Erika Krull

Approximately 42.6 million adults over age 45 in the United States are estimated to be suffering from chronic loneliness, according to AARP's Loneliness Study.

And, U.S. census data shows more than a quarter of the population lives alone, more than half of the population is unmarried and, since the previous census, marriage rates and the number of children per household have declined.

"These trends suggest that Americans are becoming less socially connected and experiencing more loneliness," said Julianne Holt-Lunstad, Ph.D.

For generations who now live and feel alone, sociality can require mental and physical preparation.

"When I force myself to attend social functions I feel so much better! I love being around people, but my anxiety and depression can get in the way. But I feel so much better when I give myself a pep talk and get myself out there!" -- Michelle Poll

"I had to practice going out; preparing myself before I left and making sure I had time when I got back to calm down. I was taught tools like deep breathing, focusing on calming my system when I talked to people, and knowing how high my anxiety was so I knew what I could handle. The more I was able to be around people when anxious, the lower my depression was. I still struggle and I have a difficult time making friends. I have only one person who I can rely on which is my husband. He is always there, understands the situation, and helps me calm down and know I'm not alone." -- Sandi Rytting

Knowing that even one person is there for you can be a remembrance that connection is real and powerful. You are part of something larger than yourself. You are part of the human race.

THE CONNECTION OF MAN

My life was never merely mine.
Nor is your life merely yours.
We owe our lives to others.
An in our daily living, we live together,
connected to the people around us.
They occupy our thoughts and inform our feelings,
and we speak their words through our lips.
We are conversing, even through our silence.
For our hearts are ever sending messages upon the wind."
-- *The Seven Paths*, by the Anasazi Foundation

REACH OUT

All kinds of social interaction are beneficial when we are suffering. We need both the reminder that we are not alone, and the acceptance of knowing we are loved. Being with babies, young children, and caring individuals can give us a sense of belonging and inclusion. Though women tend to be more social (biology shows that on the 23rd chromosome, women have an additional 1,020 genes, which likely creates the need for social bonds), all people have an innate need for social interaction. Sociality is the basis for prolongment of the human species. When you are caving in, reach out.

PRESS ON.

Quick Sociality Can-Do Tips:

- Send an emoji or simple "Thinking about you" note.
- Give a compliment. It is a kindness that is well-received and usually sparks a conversation or story.
- Make small talk (with the neighbor, cashier or mailman).
- Smile. It invites kindness and eases conversation.
- Practice socializing in safe zones. Ask for help from a librarian or store employee, someone who will respond positively to your request for social engagement.
- Look people in the eyes.
- Hold a baby. (Babies show unconditional love and react positively to touch and engagement.)
- If you are nervous to interact, text first. Plan a time to talk, so you can prepare mentally.
- Join a group or club that encourages regular attendance and interaction.
- Call a family member or trusted person and ask them to accompany you to a social engagement.
- Go to the mall or grocery store, just to be around people. (If crowds overwhelm you, choose an appropriate location with fewer people.)

CHAPTER 18:
Animal Endorphins

Animals are people, too. Right? When you see dogs dressed in princess outfits, wearing diapers, and being pushed around in strollers, it seems some of the world does believe that. And while animals are clearly not human, sociality with pets can provide some similar positive effects as time spent with people. Four legs seem to be as good as two for soothing the mind and improving mental health.

> "I have struggled with anxiety for about 10 years now. Two years ago I had a bad attack while going on a vacation. I ended up in the hospital for 3 days. My daughter thought I should have a dog. She gave me a little puppy. Now she is my little cuddle bug. She sits with me while watching TV, she follows me around and sleeps right next to me every night." -- Debbie Kidd

COOL AND CALM

Observing or being near living creatures creates fascination and induces calm (think aquariums).

> "Our dog exudes a calming energy that soothes me when I'm anxious and lifts my mood when I'm depressed." -- Sandi Rytting

Even those unable to have furry pets can enjoy the soothing benefits. Karla Montgomery says, "My son is allergic to most animal hair, but he desperately wanted a pet. We started with a small fish tank and we were amazed to watch our ADHD child sit and stare for nearly 30 minutes at a time. Now we have a turtle and lizard, in addition to our fish. Our son thrives by watching and playing with his pets. They calm his mind in a way nothing else does."

> "I was astounded that this creature was capable of the empathy that I so craved in my closest friends and relatives. It was like she could read the pathetic and sad thoughts that disabled me and wanted me to know I was lovable in the midst of my suffering.
>
> She continues to be a supportive presence in my life, especially on the days that I grow weary of trying on—and throwing out—every mindful exercise and cognitive behavioral strategy… the hours where staying positive seems impossible. She gets it. I know she does." -- Therese Borchard

A quick search on social media will tell you that people love their pets. Facebookers post nearly as many photos of animals and pets as they do of people. Some individuals identify so strongly with their animals that their pet photo is the face for their profile.

ACCEPTANCE

Animals offer near unconditional acceptance, even when our behavior wouldn't merit love from people. They accept when we confide in them, holding our secrets, while allowing us to release them out-loud. Pets offer love without the complexities and requirements of human relationships. In the process of confiding, we may also pet animals, giving us the positive benefits of touch and interaction, which include greater calm, improved mental and physical health, and fewer sick days.

> "Nothing makes me happier than my best friend!!! I know (my dog) Bailee is always there for me even if no one else is. She knows my feelings that even I don't know. I can tell her things I can't tell other people. I know she would never betray me. She is literally my BEST friend." -- Tawni Weston

FAMILY BONDS

With animals, like people, we develop strong bonds when we interact and live together in familial situations. We come to depend on each other and feel more confidence in ourselves when we are in the presence of our furry friends. Pets provide more consistency than humans, as there are fewer factors involved in the relationship.

"My pup comforts me when I am sad and will push her head under my arms while I am kneeling in prayer. She is very sensitive of my emotional needs. She also helps with anxiety.

My kitty is also good at sensing when I need love and will insist on being held.

My 12 year-old loves his guinea pig because it loves and trusts him unconditionally.

Even our chickens bring us joy when we step outside and they run up hoping for treats." -- Jamie Neff

RESPONSIBILITY AND DEPENDENCE

Animal ownership teaches encourages responsibility, as we must provide for the basic life needs of a pet. Animals remind us when they need to be taken out, fed, or when they need sleep. They can be effective for keeping us on track and encouraging activities of self-care. Routines, like waking up, eating, and going for walks, positively trigger our brains, making the tasks easier to do in the future. They depend on us—and we grow to depend on them.

Pets also help us create bonds with others; they put us around people with whom we can interact. People or not, animals are good for lifting the soul.

PRESS ON.

Quick Can-Do Animal Tips:

- Cuddle with a pet.
- Visit a pet store and play with the animals.
- Go to a petting zoo, public farm, or zoo.
- Take a dog for a walk. If you don't have a dog, offer to take the neighbor's dog.
- Go crazy and get a cat (or two). Cats are independent creatures, but they (usually) love a little love.
- Get a small fish tank or bowl; a beta fish requires little effort or equipment.
- Feed the birds. Get a small bird feeder or birdhouse for your yard or apartment deck.
- Listen to the animals and creatures in your neighborhood. Pick out the sounds of the crickets, birds, squirrels, and other wildlife.
- Go to a park and observe the wildlife.
- Plant a butterfly bush to attract winged art.

(Pet ownership should not be taken lightly. Make appropriate plans and considerations before taking on the responsibility of caring for an animal.)

CHAPTER 19:

Music

"A few notes of the song, 'This is the Time', by Billy Joel, and I time travel back 20 years and 6,000 miles. When I hear 'O, L'amour', by Erasure, I am suddenly 15 years old again, dragging Main Street with my sister in the old Buick," says Jodi Orgill Brown. Music has a way of capturing a moment, a mood, or an activity, and forever gluing them into a song.

But memories are not all that is attached to music; emotions, physical movement, and mental stimulation also accompany the beats of songs, and the effect is healing—and proven.

Un-Silence
by Jessica Thornton

Listening to music is now often thought of as a solitary activity.

Headphones in is usually seen as a way of shutting the rest of the world out. But truth be told, music has been and continues to be an outlet, a safe haven, for people struggling with depression. Music, even as a solitary activity, has a way of bringing people together and making people feel a little less alone. Perhaps Stevie Wonder sang it best in the song, "Sir Duke":

> Music is a world within itself
> with a language we all understand.[xvi]

Across cultures and across time, music has brought people together as a means of expression. Music is a form of art and a form of communication. Generations and societies can be characterized by their music, but so can the individual. On a much more personal level, music can shape each of us differently.

Whether listening or playing, composing or jamming, music reaches farther and faster into the soul than words alone. It has a powerful effect on the mind and body. Each of us has felt that at one time or another. Think back to a time you first heard a song that impacted you. Remember the sensation of hearing something so beautiful, so powerful, that you simultaneously wanted to share it with the whole world and also keep it to yourself. That feeling is the power of music.

People spend so much time soundtracking important, and even unimportant, moments of their lives. Engaged couples debate whether to have a DJ or a band play at their wedding. Apps like Spotify and 8tracks found success by allowing users to compile their own playlists to fit any mood. Why is it that music impacts us and matters to us the way it does?

STIMULATING SOUNDS
by Rebecca Clayson

Scientifically, music has the ability to redirect brain waves and nerve activity. In an article from Stanford News, Emily Saarman reported, "Rhythmic music may change brain function and treat a range of neurological conditions including … depression." The research showed that songs "with a strong beat stimulates the brain and ultimately causes brainwaves to resonate in time with the rhythm."[xvii] And, in a study conducted by Erkkilä et al in Finland, researchers concluded that music as therapy "can improve the mood and global functioning of people with this disorder."[xviii]

How music affects the brain is often stated as an over-simplified answer, but in reality, almost all parts of your brain are stimulated when listening to music.

Music can meet your specific needs.

- Listening sparks the auditory cortices and memory centers of your brain.
- Dancing or even merely tapping your foot to the beat

153

stimulates the motor cortex.

- Singing connects the portions of your brain that control movement and hearing.

Depending on the emotional response you have to a song, your brain will react in even more ways. If you were to take an fMRI while listening to music, your brain would light up like a Christmas tree.

What does this matter to people dealing with depression?

When depressed, certain parts of the brain, specifically the hippocampus and amygdala, have been found to shrink because of excess levels of cortisol. Stimulating all parts of the brain helps fight this effect, as well as release neurotransmitters associated with elevated levels of happiness like dopamine.

All this suggests that on a scientific level, music can help fight depression. Music therapy is in and of itself a scientific field. Closely related to psychology, music therapy focuses on the healing effects of music in both physical ailments and emotional or mental ailments such as depression.

Scientific explanations aside, music has been known to have healing effects on people struggling with depression. On an emotional level, music provides solace in a melody or a lyric.

MUSICAL ASCENT

Even if we do not realize it, we are influenced, positively or negatively, by lyrics, beats, and emotions from music.

"Years ago, as a teenager, I was driving in the car with my dad, singing a song along with the radio, 'I'm a loser ba-by, so why don't you kill me'. My dad turned to me with shock on his face and said, 'No wonder you are feeling down. Listen to the words you are saying to yourself.' I just sang along with the catchy beat; it hadn't even occurred to me that those words could impact my mood or feelings about myself.

But when you actually listen to the words of the music that is played all around, the words are so negative and self-demeaning; now I know that it gets to us, even when we don't realize it.

Music can have a calming influence or a disrupting influence. When I'm depressed, I need classical music, or songs with positive or motivating messages. Even if it is subconsciously, there is something good about listening to encouraging, uplifting, upbeat music. There is a reason everyone loves 'Fight Song'; it makes you feel like you can conquer the world. Even when we don't recognize why it is happening, good music brings out the good in people." -- Tami O. Baker

Next time a popular hit is playing on the radio, repeat the words, out loud, and decide if they are words you'd say to yourself, or your family members. If not, change the station, or delete the song from your playlist. Give yourself the advantage of consuming only music that brightens, lightens, or lifts.

MELODIC MENDING   by Jessica Thornton

Lori Conger survived the Cokeville, Wyoming, school bombing when she was 11-years-old. Thirty years later, she is still dealing with the consequences of that experience in the form of depression, anxiety, and PTSD. Music, specifically hymns and other songs that connect her to her faith, have had healing powers. She writes:

"Music has become a powerful tool in restoring peace and calming fears. When I feel I cannot bear the chaos, pressure and demands of life, I retreat to my bedroom, shut the door and lose myself in beautiful piano renditions of the sacred hymns. I close my eyes and soak in the hopeful messages of the inspired lyrics, allowing the beautiful strains of the piano to wash over me and calm all my emotions. Strength begins to flow into me as I silently focus on words such as, 'Fear not, I am with thee; oh, be not dismayed/ For I am they God and will still give thee aid/ I'll strengthen thee, help thee, and cause thee to stand/ Upheld my righteous, omnipotent hand' and 'Be still my soul; the Lord is on thy side.' The music calms my troubled heart and gives me the courage to get back up and keep trying." -- Lori Conger (Read her essay in part III)

In these moments, Lori is comforted by the words of the hymns and the love of God, which provide meaning for her and remind her that she is not alone, two things that can be critical to remember when dealing with depression.

Lori's experience with music and depression is connected to her faith and spirituality, but music helps people in non-religious ways, as well. Regardless of genre or artist, finding a song that speaks to your soul or your pain or your heart can have healing effects, no matter what circumstances you face.

MUSICAL MOVEMENT

Erin Grimley (see chapter on triggers for more on Erin's story), loves music, fast beats, and positive messages. "Music gets me dancing and helps to clear my mind. Exercise is a huge thing for me, and often that starts with the right music to get me moving."

For many people dealing with depression, including author Jodi Orgill Brown, getting out of bed is the first hurdle of the day.

> "I don't want to get out of bed. Not now. Not in a while. Not this afternoon. I want to sleep. Post brain trauma, sleep is critical for me and I can't seem to get enough of it. Getting up is the hardest part of my day. But when I wake to the words, 'Cheer up sleepy Jean', from the Monkees ('Daydream Believer'), it makes it a little easier to rise and start the day.
>
> The next step for me is to play my 'morning music' playlist and listen to my favorite upbeat songs; the fog lifts and I really wake up. My foot starts tapping and I get moving."

Another playlist can include songs with sentimental meaning to you. Don't try to avoid them; listen to them. Feel the emotions. Take yourself back to where you were when they first created meaning for you. This can be a form of catharsis, if you allow it. Laugh, cry, shout, and personally relive the memories. History has its place, just don't make it prominent enough to take over the future. (One exception is if a song, artist, or lyrics incite rage or volatility, avoid that music altogether. Don't allow the trigger to capture you.)

Mathematical Movement

Listening to classical music by the great composers is also powerful. Science has proven the positive effects on cognition, learning and recollection abilities when we listen to classical music, which is based on mathematical, rhythmic musical movements. It is hard to imagine that anyone could not be moved when listening to Pytor Tchaikovsky's "1812 Overture" cannon sequence, the piccolos and brass of John Philip Sousa's "Stars and Stripes Forever", the determined, yet whimsical, "Flight of the Bumble Bee" by Rimsky Korsakov, "Pachelbel's Canon", or even military marches like "The Marine's Hymn", or "The Armed Forces Medley". Feel the movement of the music and your brain and body will follow suit.

Press On.

Quick Music Can-Do Tips:

- Create playlists to fit a desired mood and activity level.
- Dance to your favorite song.
- Listen to your favorite hymns or spiritual songs.
- Learn a new instrument.
- Play around with an instrument and create your own music. Sit down at a keyboard and plunk the keys, or find an app that lets you create your own sounds and songs.
- Organize your music. YouTube has most music available free, and like your phone, you can organize it into categories or playlists, according to the beat and type of music, so you can choose accordingly:
  - Upbeat Dance music
  - Exercise music
  - Rock out
  - Classical (brain music)
  - Inspirational and uplifting
  - Low and slow
  - Instrumental
  - Show tunes (Broadway or movie music)
  - Motivating (patriotic music, military marches)
- Avoid music that is too heavy, or has negatively or inciting lyrics, or that cause rage or sorrow instead of peace or fun.
- Delete songs that trigger negative thoughts
- Explore your music tastes! Find new genres, bands, and artists and immerse yourself in them. (Try Pink Martini, Alex Boye, or Christopher Tin for fun, varied styles.)

CHAPTER 20:

Routines

by Camille Ballou and Jodi Orgill Brown

Intentional or not, depressed or not, life is lived through routines. Alarm goes off, shower, dress, groom, eat, drive to work, work, drive home, eat dinner, watch TV, chase kids, undress into pajamas, brush teeth, go to bed. Repeat.

It is Groundhog's Day at its finest.

The aforementioned routine could be considered a productive routine for someone with depression. But Groundhog's Day for some may simply be a change in venue from the bed to the couch or the changing of the channel at certain times of the day to catch certain programs. Day after day after day.

Routines add structure to our lives and make us feel comfortable and in control. They give us a sense of normalcy. And for those with depression, even the normalcy of a negative or self-destructive routine provides comfort and security.

What you do with most of your time will eventually define you. Someone who runs every day is a runner. Someone who works 20-hours a day is a workaholic. Someone who fishes is a fisherman. Someone who paints is a painter.

"The secret of your future is hidden in your daily routine", says Mike Murdock, author of The Law of Recognition. Anyone, whether depressed or not, can benefit from a positive daily routine. However, for those with depression, a routine needs to be a deliberate choice. Depression can make it difficult to simply get out of bed at all, but having a routine that begins to feel automatic can reduce the time and energy that is exerted on this simple, but critical task. Once out of bed, it becomes easier to take the next step. To shower. To groom. To feed yourself. Perhaps even exercise.

"The secret is: There is no secret ingredient to make life easier. But by doing the little things each day, we can find the daily satisfaction to keep going. If 'Kung Fu Panda' taught us anything, it is that the only secret ingredient is believing in yourself. Wake, believe, do, repeat." -- Jodi Orgill Brown

Sequence and Timing

It is important to remember that negative routines took time to develop, and so will positive routines. Dyany Munson gives the following example in relation to her depression and routines.

"I tend to be a black-and-white, all-or-nothing thinker. Many of us with depression are. When I was young, I didn't realize how devilish this could be. There was good, or there was bad, and there really wasn't much of anything in between. Have you ever noticed that if you travel a certain route over and over again, the route seems to get shorter and shorter? Or if you are trying to give directions on that route, you don't realize that the time and length from point A to point B is actually much longer than it seems? This happens to me all the time, because my brain tends to gloss over the things that are seemingly unimportant to the journey. No, I didn't notice mileposts 2, 3, 4, 5, 6, 7, or 8 because I turn at 9 and that is the important one.

But you can't get to milepost 9 if you don't pass the others. I've had a lot of setbacks over the years, and most of them I can attribute to all-or-nothing thinking. For example, I tried to eat better and I exercised for a whole week and I didn't lose any weight. This will never work! I did my physical therapy exercises three of the twelve times I was supposed to do them today. I don't feel any better. Physical therapy is dumb. Why can't I just take a pill or get surgery to fix it?

But God gave me this great thing in my life called Depression. No. Really. Depression does some dumb stuff, but the great thing is that it put me in counseling. And counseling is slowly, carefully, teaching me

160

the tools I need, along with some accountability, to make some progress. One of the most important things I'm realizing is that it takes small and simple routines in order for the great things to be realized. It is by doing the neck, shoulder and arm exercises many times a day—every day—that my arms and neck and shoulders will heal and strengthen and the pain will stop. It is by watching what I eat and exercising a bit more every day that I will lose the weight. Don't discount mileposts 2, 3, 4, 5, 6, 7, or 8. Without them it is impossible to get to 9." -- Dyany Munson (Read her essay in part III)

ONE STITCH AT A TIME

Once the small mileposts have been passed during the day, like showing, eating, cleaning, cooking or exercising, another important component of a daily routine is a hobby and some me-time.

"Life is demanding. It always will be, no matter your circumstances. I found that it was much easier to serve and nurture my children, to perform well at my job, to get out of bed and clean the house, to cook a meal, or whatever else life wanted from me at the time if I had taken some me-time. Do something simple that will fill your emotional cup, if only a little at a time." -- Camille Ballou

Dyany Munson analogized the hobby of knitting that she developed with the importance of taking small steps and having a routine.

"A ball of yarn is not super useful or pretty by itself. Its beauty and usefulness is in its potential. Different yarns have different potentials depending on their color, weight, yardage and blend. Just about any yarn can be made into just about anything, but of course its potential is maximized when used for the type of thing it was created for. But to make something out of yarn, requires more than the yarn itself. It requires proper tools, patterns and instructions. When you pick and start a project, you are picturing the end product. That is the goal. But along the way there are thousands, maybe even millions, of stitches. With knitting I have learned that each individual stitch is a joy, because each and every stitch is vital to the end goal. As I stitch and stitch, I am having fun because I am thinking about how wonderful the end product will be. I know how important each stitch is so I know I'm not wasting my time." -- Dyany Munson

A scheduled activity time or hobby helps with the healing process and gives you a safe, treasured time to look forward to.

> "I will never forget the arts and crafts time in the hospital. I thought it was stupid—a room full of psych ward patients being forced to make beaded bracelets and necklaces. I remember picking out the letters to spell each of my kid's names. I remember creating a pattern with the colors to fill in the spaces between the letters. I remember stringing the beads together and creating something I could give my children when I finally got to go home.
>
> Most of all, I remember my mind being distracted for that hour block of time and forgetting that I was depressed, forgetting to feel sorry for myself. On top of the relief I got from my depressive thoughts, I found joy in making and giving things to others.
>
> Working with my hands became better than any therapy or pill I had ever taken and I knew I needed to find an outlet, a hobby, to occupy my mind for a little while each day." -- Camille Ballou (Read her essay in part III)

A WINNING ROUTINE

Think a routine just means you are boring? Consider the connection between routines, repetition, and accomplishing goals. The world's all-time most decorated Olympian, Michael Phelps, credits his routine as his gold maker. He not only has routines for training, preparing, and competing, he rigorously sticks to them. One training streak included 1,800 straight days in the water, birthdays, Sundays, Thanksgiving, and Christmas included. He knew each time he completed his training routine, he was moving closer to achieving his goals.[xix]

A routine, especially a morning routine, will create a positive path for you to move through the milestones of healing depression. Eventually, each deliberate step from one through nine will simply become one and then nine; you will arrive at your destination without realizing how you got there.

Take some me-time and develop a hobby. Like the adage "you are what you eat," your routines shape who you are. Take time to explore things that interest you, enhance those hobbies you already have, learn and try whatever comes to mind. Allow an outlet into your routine that will stockpile your reserves and place your depressive thoughts aside, offering reprieve, if only for a time.

PRESS ON.

Quick Routine Can-Do Tips:

- Begin with a get-out-of bed routine. Set an alarm in another room, play your favorite song, or roll out of bed and get on your knees, but make it an intentional tradition.
- Don't break your date. (Practice following-through with the schedule you set for yourself.)
- Start with one thing, from the first thing you do when you get out of bed to the way you make your breakfast. Do it the same way every day for a week. Each week, add one more task to your schedule.
- Choose an activity you cherish and turn it into a daily tradition (your morning cup of tea or a walk at lunch).
- Turn a task into a routine. Take laundry time and make it into a treasured tradition, instead of a pile of hopelessness. Listen to music, dance, sing or recall favorite memories as you load, switch, and fold.
- Schedule it. Turn chaos into order by putting time on the calendar to complete your everyday tasks.
- Schedule time for things you love, self-care, or spending time with your loved ones. Integrate them into your routine.
- Give yourself a serotonin rush by acknowledging the routines you already have. (Look at even the little things such as your commute, getting ready for bed, etc.)
- Schedule a pay (bills) day, and a play day every week.
- Set your schedule to music.

CHAPTER 21:
Physical Activity

by Camille Ballou and Brandon T. Orgill

"Exercise gives you endorphins. Endorphins make you happy. Happy people just don't shoot their husbands, they just don't." Or so says Elle Woods in the movie *Legally Blonde*.

A person with depression longs for a happiness that seems to elude them—the kind of happiness that Elle Woods explains so eloquently. The kind of happiness that Elle firmly believes is in direct correlation to exercise.

But a depressed individual reading these words is tempted to stop reading altogether. She is tempted to shut the book on the words contained in this chapter. She is likely feeling frustration and anxiety rise at the mere implication, because exercise is one of the hardest prescriptions to fill.

When suffering from depression, we often neglect ourselves physically in some manner out of the necessity to survive on an emotional level. We lack the self-confidence and motivation required to begin, and ultimately sustain, an exercise regime.

But the physical barriers are not the ones that need to be overcome. When you factor in the emotional and mental barriers, it feels like David standing at the feet of Goliath, without a slingshot. It simply cannot be done. But champion golfer Arnold Palmer promised, "The most rewarding things you do in life are often the ones that look like they cannot be done."[xx]

So what are the rewards of exercise and physical activity? Why should it matter to the healing process of depression? How does someone with depression become convinced that it is worth the effort involved? And that, despite the thoughtless comments or suggestions of, "Go outside more!" or "You just need to exercise!" you may have received in the past, there is some merit?

Just ask Elle Woods.

CHEMICAL FITNESS

Depression is a complex mood disorder. While life and our experiences and circumstances can perpetuate the disorder, your brain biochemistry usually plays a dominant role.

Sufferer Brandon Orgill acknowledged, "Exercise is absolutely essential when dealing with depression. I love to work out and, for the most part, I've been good about being consistent with my regime. The times when I didn't work out, my depression worsened. Sometimes I didn't work out *because* I was depressed. Other times I stopped working out due to injury. Looking back, I wish I'd continued to do what I could instead of using injuries or depression as an excuse to take time off altogether. On top of the endorphin rush, you also get long-term benefits in overall brain function, as it suppresses naturally created chemicals which may worsen depression."

Rebecca Clayson states, "On a daily basis, there are many things people with depression can do to combat symptoms. These involve utilizing the naturally occurring chemicals in the body and brain in a constructive way. Exercise releases endorphins—positive chemicals; energizing chemicals."

Let's explore the chemical effects of exercise that Brandon, Rebecca and of course, Elle, have mentioned.

RELEASING FEEL-GOOD BRAIN CHEMICALS

The feel-good brain chemicals that are released with exercise contribute to what is commonly known as a "runner's high." When you physically exert yourself, your brain releases endorphins. Endorphins are a type of neurotransmitter, or chemical messenger.

They aid in pain and stress relief. While they are the most famous of the neurotransmitters released when you exercise, they are not the only ones. Exercise also stimulates the release of dopamine, norepinephrine, and serotonin, all of which play an important role in regulating mood. In fact, many medications on the market that treat depression attempt to balance the levels of serotonin and other neurotransmitters. (See section on happy hormones for more information.)

REDUCING IMMUNE SYSTEM CHEMICALS & STRESS HORMONES

While depressed individuals have heard of endorphins ad nauseam, to the point of them being reduced to a four-letter word, the lesser known chemical benefits of exercise lie within the reduction of certain harmful chemicals and stress hormones, such as adrenaline and cortisol. Adrenaline plays a role in your fight-or-flight responses and gives you the immediate energy boost to face (or run from) danger. But too much of it can become harmful to your emotional health. Cortisol, which regulates metabolism, is also known is the "stress hormone," reduces serotonin and other neurotransmitters, including dopamine.

Research also indicates the immune system is highly involved with psychiatric diseases like depression. Most medications are prescribed to balance the aforementioned feel-good chemicals in the brain, and regular exercise is known to strengthen the immune system.

Fika Mariana has Bell's Palsy and learned long ago the positive effects of pushing her body to release the stress in her mind.

> "I go out to do sports with others; I make myself as tired as I can so I am too tired to deal with negative thoughts. I've joined an athletic club, basketball team, swimming team, and taekwondo. I kick as hard as I can, I run as fast as I can. It's just the time I release the scream in me. Sometimes I cry and I sweat, and no one knows. My muscles aching and burning and feeling the pain—that is when I know I am alive and kicking." – Fika Mariana

PHYSICAL FITNESS

Bodies in motion tend to stay in motion and bodies at rest tend to stay at rest. Trust Isaac Newton on this one, who introduced the world to the First Law of Motion: Inertia. A spinning wheel will keep spinning until acted upon by an outside force, or until friction (also from an outside source) slows it down.

If for no other reason, get your body moving so you are moving, rather than sitting, laying, or vegging in your cave. Vacuum. Walk the dog. Go get the mail. Take the garbage out. Even the simplest acts of movement can start our bodies moving. Our bodies are not meant to be sedentary. Thousands of years of evolutionary development required humans to move to survive—and that cannot disappear in a few generations of ease. Never before in the history of the world have people had to move so little in order to survive. The very functions of the body require that we move in order to stay healthy. Fat stores grow when we stop moving, digestion slows, metabolism slows, the immune system weakens, and we actually lose energy. If you feel like you have no energy, MOVE. You may think you need to rest, but the opposite is true.

> "Start with very small steps that may not work out very well at first. It's like trying to exercise after being bedridden. You feel like it's something that could help you feel like living, but it takes a lot of energy. I remember my parents getting me to go hiking because it always made me happy. I hated the first few times, but I found that I could do it for myself until I enjoyed it more." – Kathryn Ann Olsen

If you aren't "good" at keeping yourself going, go with science. Research has shown that people move for longer periods of time when it requires more effort for them to stop. Walking requires little effort to stop, so when given the option to stop walking, many walkers will simply cease. But individuals who were riding bikes or rowing (on machines), opted to go longer than asked or required (for the study) because it required more effort to slow, stop, and dismount.

Another option to increase your movement is to go in one direction. If you think you only want to walk for five minutes, instead, walk in one direction for five minutes. You will achieve your goal and still have the need to return, so you will log another five minutes of movement. Create a path that requires you to turn around and go back, rather than just walking around the block.

> "For me, exercise is essential. I feel better, look better, and have more energy. That energy helps me get out of bed in the morning, and the physical exertion helps me fall asleep at night when my mind, much to my chagrin, wants to run non-stop. And hey, looking our best can only help, right? Especially when we're so caught up in other issues and worries." – Brandon T. Orgill

Looking and feeling better about the reflection you see in the mirror can be a huge morale boost, which feeds the drive to maintain the regimen. Over time, improvement in your overall health and sleep patterns will naturally follow. Improved quality and quantity of sleep can vastly increase a depressed individual's ability to cope with and focus on the healing process of depression. Better sleep reduces anxiety and irritability.

The culmination of both the chemical and physical benefits of exercise should be an improvement to the depression.

- "After the birth of my daughter, I was a complete wreck. I was put on an extremely high dose of anti-depressants. I could barely stand to leave the house. Eight months later I was sitting in the doctor's office, sobbing. I was in extreme pain due to many physical ailments that had surfaced, and my depression was getting worse. After a required surgery, it struck me that I needed to get outside. From that moment on, my daughter and I were always outside. I started walking a mile or more a day and being out in the sunshine. The more time we spent outside exercising, the more my symptoms decreased. Gradually I was brought down from my very high dose of anti-depressants to the point I was finally taken off of them." – Brandi Nicole Astle

HEALTHY CONNECTION

The effects of physical activity are enhanced when participants have a partner or are part of a group. The social aspects of working together and just being together, induce positive, hormone-releasing highs.

> "After my husband died, my workout friends became my lifeline. When I run with them, I am releasing my stress and sadness, and I am

surrounded by support. It is the perfect combination." – Linda*

But you don't need to be part of a group of runners, Crossfit fanatics, or boot camp buddies to benefit from the healthy social effects of physical activity. Get out of the house and start moving, and the connections will come.

"I believe doctors should prescribe walking instead of drugs. Start by just walking around the block and build up. Soon you become familiar with neighbors, conversations are started, friends are made, and walking becomes more than just walking. It becomes healing." – Robin Cranney

Healthy Competition

There is one final benefit of exercise.

The Competition.

Or rather the challenge, the hard work, and the ultimate pay-off of competing against yourself—and maybe even someone else in a healthy, friendly way—and coming out a champion.

"I'll never forget [my] first half-marathon.

I was seventy-five pounds overweight as a result of my depression. I had to walk half and could barely jog the other half. It took me three hours. But the exhilaration. The feeling of accomplishment. The overwhelming pride I felt as the tears ran down my face when I crossed the finish line healed something inside of me." – Camille Ballou

So go ahead. Get high—on exercise, that is.

Press On.

Quick Exercise Can-Do Tips:

- Walk to work, school, or the grocery store.
- Take the stairs (instead of the elevator), or run the stairs at home for a quick heart-rate bump.
- Go for a run with a friend. (Going with a friend makes you accountable to that individual, creates sociality, builds trust, and gets you moving.)
- Take the garbage out.
- Ride a bike. Has it been a while? Get on and start pedaling and you'll remember the joy you had riding a bike as a kid.
- Walk the dog.
- Turn on music and just start dancing.
- Grab a ball and start tossing, kicking, throwing, or bouncing.
- Sign up for a class at your community or recreation center. (Many communities offer free or low-cost classes for locals.)
- Stretch. Simple yoga poses stretch and strengthen the body and require nothing more than a few feet of floor space.
- Jumping jacks get your heart pumping and your body ready to start moving.

PART III

PERSONAL ESSAYS OF STRENGTH DURING THE RISE

Part III is a series of personal essays and reflections written by those who suffer. The reflections, insights, and storytelling are their own. These brave warriors, like you, strive to rise above depression every day. While no one will ever live in your shoes, find strength and comfort in the vulnerability, progress, lessons, and hope they share. May these essays open your heart and enlarge your capacity to endure and rise.

CHAPTER 22:
Death of the Funny Man

by Brandon T. Orgill

Robin Williams died yesterday. [July 21, 1951 - August 11, 2014]

The world rarely shows such an incredible outpouring for the death of one individual. So what does it say when news coverage, Twitter, Facebook, and Instagram are utterly inundated by cries of love and respect for this man and his work? He was loved. He was admired. He made people smile. He made people feel.

Feel. I relate to this word, to this concept. For someone living with, battling, fighting, struggling, and often losing to depression, I understand the word "feel" far too well. I think, perhaps, that Robin Williams was the same.

You see, depression, real, lasting, non-circumstantial depression, at its very core, is a problem of feeling. Sure, yes, it's misfiring synapses and chemical imbalances in the brain . . . but at its core— at my core—it's a problem with feeling. Feeling too much about the wrong things. It means having a difficult, almost impossible struggle to control feeling. To me, that's depression.

Robin Williams was, by all measurable means, a man who ought to have been happy and beyond such struggles. He had everything he needed to stay alive without undue anxiety or stress. He had personal and non-personal love almost unendingly showered in his direction. He had laughter, fun, and what often seem like happiness, despite his well-documented struggles with personal demons. And yet he's dead. He hit his limit, for whatever reason. Game over.

Depression.

Depression, true, lasting, crippling depression is hard to define. I've often compared it to describing the color of the sky to a blind person. How could anyone who hasn't/doesn't experience it ever really understand? People go through hardships, a bad break-up, being laid off, the death of loved ones, and they feel depression, anxiety, fear . . . but it's temporary. Time heals all wounds, as they say. But true depression, time doesn't heal it. You either find a way to make yourself strong enough to battle it, or it takes you. There's no gray area here. Depression kills. Unless, of course, we find a way to keep it from killing us.

I hope by now it's readily apparent this is a topic with which I share a fair amount of familiarity. I've been hospitalized for suicide attempts. I've lived with depression. I've fought and I've momentarily lost. I continue to fight. And people, most people, continue to not understand. They want to, that much is obvious, but they've never seen the color of the sky. There are no words that can help them understand. It does little to explain to them what it's like to experience their worst, most debilitating life events and have that as an on-going undercurrent in their lives, indefinitely.

This is my life. Was this Robin Williams' life?

Some people who experience depression find fame and fortune. They are loved, they create wonderful things, only to find it's not enough. It's the tragic link between creativity, intelligence, and depression. You get Kurt Cobain, Robin Williams, Heath Ledger, and Elvis Presley, among others. People who ought to have been or were titans. And yet they fall.

I don't know fame. I certainly don't know fortune. At times I actively shun and avoid many of the aspects of life that could lead me in that direction simply because it means letting down protective walls I've put in place to keep myself safe. I'm most creative, most actively productive when I'm at my worst, as counter-intuitive as that seems. I produce page after page, I write songs and blogs and... and I try... because that effort, that expression, that hope of something more, of something better, is all that keeps my head above water.

I actively keep myself mundane, ordinary, less productive because it hurts less. And then I hate myself for not producing, for not building, for not being something more.

I wish there were a simple, easy way to wrap this up, some magical answer to depression, a secret coping tool to share with the world. But as far as I'm aware, there's not. And I'm here. Writing this. And another battle has been lost and a great warrior has passed on. We will miss you, Mr. Williams.

I don't expect anyone to understand. I don't expect anyone to really comprehend unless it's something they do battle with. But awareness, now that's something. Who knows what might be different if people were aware, if those with depression were completely and honestly open in their darkest hours? Who would still be alive? What works would we have that we don't?

No, I don't expect anyone to understand. But to try. To feel. Well, there's an amazing amount of power in feeling.

Feel.

PRESS ON.

RISE.

(Note: This is one of two essays by Brandon T. Orgill. See his author bio at the end of chapter 23.)

CHAPTER 23:
The Battle Against Entropy

by Brandon T. Orgill

I live with true, deep-seeded depression. I'm not talking about feeling down and out after a break-up or the death of a loved one. I mean a constant battle of will, every single day.

But let me bypass the explanations that will not and cannot convey what I mean and how I feel, and instead state it truly and simply:

In the last decade, I can count on one hand the number of days during which I haven't thought about and seriously considered suicide.

I can name each of those days, describe exactly what happened, and tell you exactly what I thought and felt the next morning upon realizing I'd gone one blissful day without the thought touching my mind.

I'm not proud of this, but I'm not ashamed. I certainly do not actively choose to broadcast this fact to the world, because, plain and simple, most people just have no clue how to deal with such an admission. This is just a fact, a cold hard reality, no more and no less.

Though I've tried in the past to explain the whys of my situation, my thoughts and feelings, I'll bypass them. I can't describe them to my own satisfaction, nor, I've found, to anyone else's, either. Instead, let me skip to the effects this has had on my life and the certain consequences of all these things.

178

DAILY EFFECTS OF DEPRESSION

First and foremost, I will say this has affected my ability to sleep, which as most people know, only compounds any mental issues or stress you're already dealing with. On average, I would say I probably get a solid two or three hours of sleep a night, at most. It is not unusual for me to spend four or five hours simply wishing I could fall asleep. But I find myself unable to do so, even though I'm mentally and physically exhausted. My brain simply will not shut off, the cogs will not stop turning. Nothing I've found or tried has had any lasting impact on this. And falling asleep is only a part of the problem. Once I've fallen asleep I can rarely stay asleep for more than a couple of hours without waking up.

As you might imagine, having a difficult time falling asleep and staying asleep, has a very adverse effect upon my mornings. As if it weren't enough to have a mental battle to go through to convince myself to get out of bed, no matter how rested I feel, most days I find I have to battle complete exhaustion in addition to my mental morning routine of arguing with myself about the reasons death is preferable to getting out of bed.

As a direct result of my sleeping issues, and the depression on top of them, I've found it is very hard for me to be truly reliable in any form before noon, and not even always by then. I simply have never found any reason or occasion that has had the significance or influence to constantly and continuously get me out of bed when I have obligations. I hate this. I try very hard to be a very hard working and reliable person. I pride myself on my ability to excel, indeed, to come out on top in nearly any form of competition. And I view nearly everything in life as some form of competition or another (call it a mental game that lends me a certain amount of motivation where there might otherwise be none).

Because I've been unable to make or will myself into morning reliability, I've actively developed and sought after skill sets and interests which might allow me to live and hopefully someday make a living in which my morning and sleep issues simply won't be an important factor.

INSATIABLE NEEDS

Helping Others

Interestingly, my depression has caused many of my best qualities to grow and to flourish. Though I will not pretend to be the nicest or most considerate person in the world, I have found I have an insatiable need to help people who feel down or who are having problems. To put it simply, I cannot stand the thought of someone else sharing in the type of misery I wake up with and fall asleep to every day. I will go out of my way to help someone I sense is in need. This has also made me loyal to those I consider my friends in ways that, I've found, seem to bypass what most people would consider normal or prudent. I will, in point of fact, help someone I care about regardless of any personal pain or discomfort it might cause me. I am, as I think I've made clear, already depressed. What is a little more pain and sadness if I can help someone else?

The Power of Creation

As you might expect, I have not found contentment in regards to my mental state. I am not happy to be depressed, and therefore I have aggressively and ceaselessly striven to find ways to manage my depression and to hopefully one day overcome it. I have tackled the complexities of religion, both organized and otherwise. I've pondered over and experimented with the many facets of social and personal relationships, and I have done anything and everything else I can possibly think of. I can say, with a perfect certainty, that I have found only two things in my life upon which I can rely entirely to help increase my personal happiness: Making people happy (vague, I know), and creating *something*.

I'm here to focus on creation. It is an odd thing to realize I managed to work my way through a college degree with little personal satisfaction and feeling much as if I were wasting my time, only to find that ten minutes of writing a story or essay can entirely change my mood for the better. I can work myself half to death and feel none better for it, and yet I can write a piece of music, which hardly anyone will ever hear and be perfectly content. (Forget for a moment that these other things are a form of creation

180

and realize that I mean they are not the type of creation I long for.)

I won't pretend to understand why creation seamlessly and effortlessly allows me to overcome depression when very little can have any noticeable difference. Call it deep-set, intrinsic, human nature—or anything else you might. The reasons don't matter to me as much as the results. And the results, ultimately, are satisfaction and happiness. Two goals that I think I can safely say, everyone desires.

Creation bears with it a certain power and mystique. *Making something from nothing and building something that is greater than the sum of its parts has a certain power to it.*

If you care to look at it from a scientific standpoint, you can say everything in existence is slowly going the path of chaos. That is to say, entropy is a natural law, whereby everything, sooner or later, degrades to its simplest state; things break down. The only thing standing between ultimate chaos—complete entropy—is sentient beings using their own personal energy to create.

On a day-to-day level, I would say any given person does very little to contribute to the battle against entropy. Indeed, that seems a task slated for God and angels alone. I cannot organize matter and shape the world to my will, at least not to any grand extent. And yet, I have the power within me to build a house, to write a song or story, or to create a business. By doing one of these things, I can create. I can overcome the natural laws that say all things must decay. And it is this creation that lends me satisfaction and happiness. I am battling against something, and it is a personal battle I certainly want to win.

It might seem odd to think of creation in terms of battling chaos, but when your mind is a mess of depression, you think deeply on many things and come to ideas and conclusions people might find intriguing or weird. But I truly believe it is this battle against chaos, darkness, Satan, or whatever you choose to call it, that grants satisfaction and happiness.

Creation is my ultimate tool for personal happiness. By creating we progress, the world becomes better and brighter, something that might have been nothing now becomes something, and happiness flourishes. A better you, a poem, a house, a business, art, it doesn't matter what you create; it simply matters that you *do* create, and you do so with purpose and design.

Progression is the goal and creation is a vehicle to get you there.

The truly amazing and incredible thing about progression is that it is a goal that cannot be reached. It is a task that must be done continuously or it fails. We must create, we must grow, continuously, or we, and our happiness, will ultimately fail.

I believe the true key is determining in what ways you excel or desire to create something, and then cultivating that talent and desire by actively working to create whatever you want, even if it is a hundred little things.

I live and battle with severe depression. I will not pretend that my life and my mental state will instantly and magically change for the better by creating something. Life is not so simple as that. But creation is my tool of choice. Continuous progression is my goal. Maybe if you put those definitions to work in your life, you might find the type of results that make your days brighter and happier than they would otherwise be.

PRESS ON.

RISE.

About the Author: Brandon T. Orgill is a writer with an eclectic assortment of widely varying experiences, skills, and expectations. Find him online at: http://abucketofrandomness.blogspot.com/

CHAPTER 24:
The Journey's Destination

by Kristy Jo Hunt

If someone had told me in my early twenties that I would someday be 100% off my anti-depressant medication, have the skills and mindset strength to encounter difficult situations with joy, and have the habits and knowledge of how to fuel and train my body to be my greatest asset in positive moods, I would have thought they were crazy.

But here I am, ten years in front of the girl who had no control, who was a victim of her body, her mind, and her medications. The journey's destination was not known at the time I started it. I just knew I wanted control. I wanted power. I wanted hope. I had none of those things, and I learned to walk from principle to principle with blinders on, a laser-focused goal-oriented attitude that often blinded me to the lives that others live around me.

Now, I can honestly say the pain of those years was worth it. I have more understanding and absolute respect for the way God helps us work through our challenges. He sees them as opportunities. It's our job to learn *why* He needs us to work through them. There is no benefit in masking the pains and struggles. There is no saving us from them. It's part of the plan. Yes, the agony and feelings of anger rise high. For me, they rose for years on end. I distanced myself from God. I turned my back and rebelled for resentment and anger at the cross He had given me to bear. Surely, He could have chosen something easier? Surely, He didn't think I was capable of getting through *all those things,* did He?

183

Yes, He did. And He was there with me every step of the way. He was there with me while I cursed His name. He was there with me, enlightening me with knowledge and inspiration when I dared to ask for help. He created bridges for me when my own bridge from one destination to the next was too short. It was His extended hand that saved me, after empowering me to push and become and learn and try with all of the power I had, then extending my power to finish it, as mine was not enough.

That is the power of learning to master the vehicle of the body. Nutrition, Fitness, Mindset, Emotions, and Spirit . . . it's all interrelated. My journey is far from over, but my, oh my, every time He offers me a view at where I have come from to where I am now, I marvel in awe at His great, glorious plan and wisdom.

PRESS ON.

RISE.

About the Author: Kristy Jo Hunt is a Mind and Body Strategist who specializes in Women's Autoimmune Conditions and Emotional Eating Recovery. Find her online at PowerFoodsLifestyle.com

CHAPTER 25:
The Monster and Me

by Blen W. Harline

Going day to day with depression takes a lot of strength. Strength over our emotions, over our impulses, strength to smile when we don't feel it, and most days, strength to even get out of bed. I sometimes try to imagine what it would be like to go through the day without a care. It's depressing!

Pun intended. I was diagnosed with Clinical Depression after about four years in the Army Reserves. I had just started a new job working for the Army Reserves as a civilian. It was quite a blow to my confidence and caused a lot of uncertainty about what would happen with my career. I wish I would have known that I was not alone in feeling these things and that I could be successful even while dragging along my emotional baggage; feeling alone and uncertain made things harder to deal with.

That's why I ultimately decided to write this. Knowing that regular, everyday people achieve success while bearing this burden can go pretty far in helping one cope. Being in the military, you are constantly evaluated. You are routinely corrected when you do wrong and complimented when you do well, and your leaders don't soften things to protect your feelings.

FACE VALUE

The problem was that even on my best days, what I heard from my leaders and what my depression told me were often in glaring contrast. They saw much more in me than my depression let me see in myself. I started to view depression as my inner monster that loved nothing more than to lie to me. I have learned to cage it, and even though I can still hear it complaining in the background, I don't have to look at it. It prevents me from seeing so many things that make daily life easier. I know this sounds a little disconnected, like I have forgotten that the monster is actually me, but follow me on this, and I think it will make sense as we go along.

As I became more aware of my depression, it became clear that any time I was given a compliment, my initial reaction was to question the source. Did they really mean it? Were they just trying to be nice? Was it pity? Was it sarcasm? Did they gain anything by making me feel good?

My first real step toward living with depression was when I decided that no matter what, I would take compliments at face value. I decided that the monster (depression) often spoke nonsense. Once I began to recognize this, I sought to ignore it.

Now is about the time you say, "Easier said than done. You should hear how loud my monster is!"

You are right. Ignoring it is about as easy as ignoring construction right outside your bedroom window. So what's the secret to silence the noise? Simply stated, there isn't one.

JUMPING THE HURDLES

Overcoming a hurdle does not start by pretending it is not there. I hear the taunting loud and clear, but I recognize it for what it is. I know intellectually that I have depression, and I know that what I am feeling may not necessarily be true. What I am saying is, I own it! I am not owned by an illness! I hear what the monster says and then judge whether or not it speaks the truth. If not, I disregard what it has to say. This is not a skill I have fully mastered, some days are better than others, but when I started making the effort to take compliments at face value, you can bet that dealing with the rest of the baggage became easier.

IGNORING THE BEAST

The next thing I have learned is that *even though the monster keeps telling me otherwise*, I have accomplished a lot in my life. I don't walk around telling people how successful I am, but I do acknowledge it to myself, even if I have to shout over my feelings. The thing is, before I knew I had depression, I was trying to push forward while the monster dug in its heels. When I would look back at my accomplishments, I would almost always minimize them with my internal dialogue:

"Graduated high school . . . but my grades were terrible."

"Rebuilt an engine . . . but lots of people do."

"Learned how to play an instrument, sang in choir . . . is that even a useful skill?"

"Completed basic training . . . it's still easier than Marine boot camp."

The Measuring Stick

But in reality, whatever the accomplishment was, I succeeded, even with the odds against me! Success can be measured a lot differently for someone who not only worked hard but also fought themselves every step of way. Did your accomplishment have long-standing effects on your, or another's, life?

Maybe, maybe not, but who cares? Does everything you do have to be remarkable? There are many levels of accomplishment. Some things you will do better than many people, some things not as well.

People are remembered for their greatest achievements, but you can be certain that they achieved many things that only they know about. It doesn't matter if your greatest achievement doesn't measure up to someone else's.

What Matters to the Monster

That brings me to my next point. Comparing myself to others is detrimental. I never cease to notice the strengths obvious in others that I don't have. The internal struggle takes over again:

"Look how she talks to her friends, the ease at which she can make them laugh and follow her every word."

"Look how people gravitate to that guy! Look at how handsome he is!"

The thing is, *the monster doesn't always know what actually matters to me.* It's assuming that what's important to some people and what their talents are is something I should be good at.

My depression was not letting me acknowledge my own talents and see how good I actually was at the things I am passionate about.

I have to remind myself to stop using someone else's tape measure to measure my own self-worth.

Why should I be jealous about someone doing something I wouldn't want to do anyway? This happens to me all the time. I play guitar, and I don't care to learn the drums, but I catch myself all the time feeling jealous at how good someone else is at drumming. Why do I care if someone else can play the drums and I can't? I don't care, but my depression makes me think I should. I can be good at what my talents are and let others be good at theirs. Don't get me wrong, when I decided to learn guitar, I compared my skill to other guitar players, but I keep the monster in check (some days better than others). I tell myself, "that guy is a lot better than me at guitar, but I'll get there eventually if I keep working at it. By the way, look at how much better I am than I was six months ago!" I let it push me to be better, but fought against its tendency to make me feel bad about how I was doing.

I used my own tape measure.

TO DRAG THE BEAST

The final thing I want to mention is how I get over being lethargic. As everyone with depression knows, getting yourself moving is incredibly difficult! This is one thing that even knowing it's from my depression, it still holds me back. I'll be honest, my military discipline may play a role in how I power through it, but also I have learned to look at the end state of things rather than the beginning.

Because I look for ways to compliment myself (to quiet the

monster), knowing that the end state of my actions will provide one of those compliments really helps me to get moving. I still have all the normal drives that others have: satisfaction, pride, altruism, needing success, to name a few, but I have to find ways around the struggle of beginning things. Every time I accomplish something, whether it be mowing the lawn or completing a huge project, I store away in my mind the feelings of accomplishment that comes from it to draw upon later. Even with my success in the military and being on the path to having a military and civil service retirement under my belt before I turn forty-five, this is one of the hardest things I deal with personally. Looking at the end result helps me to ignore what I have to overcome to start the project, not least of which is getting out of bed and getting myself ready and out the door.

The military uses the phrase "high speed, low drag," which is an acknowledgment when someone is making difficult things look easy. I often joke that I am "High speed, High drag," and even though I am joking, I am really not joking. I have dragged the monster along for the ride I want to go on.

COUNTING THE THINGS THAT COUNT

I am blessed to be married to an amazing woman who helps me so much in recognizing my worth. We have two incredible daughters, we live comfortably on my wages, I can see my retirement down the road, and I am a deacon and music leader at my church. To this day, I am still stunned every time I manage to speak confidently in meetings, when people come to me for a small dose of sarcastic wit, and the most frightening, when I sing in front of people.

In the grand scheme of things, I may or may not stand out as much as my depression tells me I should, but compared to the mess I was before I knew where the feelings came from, I am doing well and the best I can.

Medication helps, but sometimes I still feel the overwhelming sadness, frustration, or anger, so much so that to speak would cause it to burst out of me. Other days, I forget all about it and feel "normal." There are days when I can't seem to bring myself to do anything and other days when I can work extra hard to make up for it. It happens!

On the days when I struggle the most, I count on the support of those closest to me to help me through. **The feelings of being alone in your suffering are just feelings, not reality.** Many people go through depression, with varying levels of severity. Talking to someone who understands what you are going through is important, and reaching out when you are feeling vulnerable shows great strength. No two people suffer depression in the same way, some things that work for me may not be as useful to you, but I hope these things will either work for you or will help get you started on finding the things that do. You can achieve success, and more importantly, live happily with yourself. Lastly, always remember that Clinical Depression is an illness, not a weakness!

PRESS ON.

RISE.

About the Author: Blen W. Harline is an amateur writer, Christian singer/songwriter, father, husband, and a Soldier.

CHAPTER 26:
The Purpose of the Barbell

by Dyany Munson

Exercise and suffering—they go together, you know. Some forms of exercise have multiple purposes. For instance, walking can also serve to take you places or show you pretty things. Sports can also be competitive (if you like that sort of thing), or social, or teach teamwork, or even be fun. Yoga can be a form of relaxation and meditation. But one very hard type of exercise has only one purpose: the barbell. You know, that huge steel bar with the big weights on the ends. It ties you to gravity. It offers resistance. It is designed for one purpose and one purpose only: to be very, very hard to lift.

Life is like a gym. You go in there with a purpose: to become fit and strong. There are some visible benefits to this: maybe you want to lose some excess fat or just tone some muscles so you can look better. There are even more invisible benefits to this: get rid of fats that clog your arteries and make your organs and muscles less efficient, make your body process insulin and carbs better, release endorphins to make you happier. And there are long-term benefits as well, of having the strength and the stamina to do the things that will come up in our lives. So many times we go ONLY for the visible benefits, even though those are the ones that really matter the least. We go there with a purpose. Maybe we're clutching a tattered picture of Arnold Schwarzenegger from the 1980s, thinking, "This is what I want to look like." And we do some time on the treadmill and maybe lift some dumbbells a few times, then look in the mirror and think, "Why am I doing this? It's not very fun and I don't see any difference at all!"

Then the personal trainer comes in. His name is Jesus Christ. And he says he can help you meet the goals you set in the first place. And it's free! "Sweet," you think, "I like free stuff!" But then the real work begins. More time on the treadmill. More dumbbells. More resistance machines. And still, at the end of the day, you look at yourself and you don't see much difference.

Then come the barbells.

Holy cow, you hate those things. You avoided them before because you saw people do them on their own and either take on too much and get hurt, or take on too little and not see any progress. So why would anyone want to take them on? But this personal trainer, man, He is *hard core*. He has you doing those stupid things every single day and He is pushing you WAY beyond comfortable. You hurt. Every day, you hurt. And you still look in the mirror and it seems it's not making any difference. One day, as Christ is spotting you on those cursed barbells, you say, "I don't think I want to look like Arnold anymore. Forget it. I just want some cheesecake and a nap. I don't want to do these barbells even one more time!"

And Christ says, "Oh, you're not going to look like Arnold when we're done. You're going to look *better.*"

Because we all have trials that are just like those barbells. We see no purpose for them but the suffering. And we have seen trials destroy others who have not utilized the personal trainer we all have access to for free. When we look at ourselves in the mirror every day, we don't see the progress we are making, because it comes so slowly, bit by agonizing bit.

But if we rely on our personal trainer and His expertise in knowing how much is too much and how much is too little to give us the strength we need for things that will come up after we leave this gym, those barbells will be the biggest blessing we could ever imagine.

Because it is only through resistance that we gain strength.

PRESS ON.

RISE.

About the Author: Dyany Munson is a peer support specialist, speaker, and aspiring author. Find her online at www.dyany.com.

CHAPTER 27:
Light is Stronger than Darkness

by Kate Durtschi

It's like standing on the edge of a dark abyss. Your toes are hanging over the side, and you feel like you could fall into something deep and black and frightening at any moment.

It's like being in the ocean with the waves battering and beating you. Your footing is shaken and unsure, and you feel like the undertow could grab you any second and pull you down. You already feel like you're drowning, like at any second it will all be too much and you'll give up.

It's like standing in the face of a giant, nasty beast. One you're all too familiar with. He stands and roars in your face, making your hair blow back and your eyes close. His sharp teeth are right there, daring you to have the strength to make him stand down. He scares you, he makes you cry, he makes you feel hopeless.

Wouldn't it be easier to just give up? To step over the edge, to fall down in the waves, to give into the beast? Wouldn't it be better that way?

NO. It would not be better. Even when things seem to be at their worst, and you feel like you're at your weakest and ready to break, never back down. Never give up. You are braver and stronger and better than you think. **You're still here, you're still fighting.** It may not feel like you have any fight left in you, but I promise you that you do.

Step back from the edge, get out of the waves, and tell that beast to lay down and shut up. He may be back, but in this moment, you have won. You have made him cower. And you will do it again. It is so hard and so overwhelming, but you always keep fighting and don't you ever give up. Because as hard and painful and lonely as this life can be, it is worth it. There is joy and beauty and love in small moments. Don't give that up. You are better and stronger than giving up. You may get knocked down, but just keep getting back up. You are worth fighting for even if you're the only one doing the fighting right now. You are worth it. You are precious. Your life is precious. Never give it up. You are in charge of you, and you decide to stay. Give it everything you have in you, even if all you have in you is one more minute, one more hour, one more day, and then give some more.

You were not meant for darkness and despair. **You were meant for light and joy. Look for the light—it will come. I promise. Light is stronger than darkness.**

PRESS ON.

RISE.

About the Author: Kate Durtschi earned a BA in English from BYU and is an Army veteran, a wife, a mother of four, and a writer.

CHAPTER 28:
The Most Important Lesson

by Rebecca Clayson

A few weeks after my second child was born, a brief conversation with a total stranger left me despondent. I expected the melancholy to pass since I'd had similar experiences before but, as the days and weeks passed, I became consumed with despair and sadness. It was difficult to function. My mind was in a fog, and I didn't really feel part of the world. I would curl into a ball and cry for hours. Some days I forced cheerfulness and tried to be perfect at everything in hopes of dispelling the gloom. When that didn't work, I would feel angry, ashamed, and embarrassed by my worthlessness. I lost hope and felt that my life had no meaning.

I didn't share what I felt with anyone, including my husband, because I was afraid they would only confirm my fears: that I was incapable of being a good wife and mother; that it would be better for someone else to take my place.

Thinking my sorrow could be caused by sin, I sought counsel from my ecclesiastical leader. I hoped confessing, even though I hadn't done anything major to confess, might lift the weight of sadness. When talking with him didn't help, I felt even worse. Why had God abandoned me? Where was the love that was supposed to be unconditional? What had I done to offend Him? I prayed daily, asking for forgiveness and pleading for peace to be restored to my soul. I read the scriptures and other inspiring words; I listened to uplifting music. Nothing combated the intense melancholy. The despair was almost unbearable.

I rode this roller coaster of emotion for nearly a year before a neighbor told me she thought I had depression. At first I was offended. I was hurting, not crazy. Not only that, I had a degree in health education and a minor in psychology. I *knew* what depression was. But the more she described the symptoms of depression, the more I saw myself in her words. I was stunned to realize that what felt like a spiritual battle of self-worth was really a form of mental illness.

That's when I also realized I *didn't* understand depression as well as I thought I did. Part of the reason for this may have been that few people talk about it and, when they do, it is often in hushed tones. Even after my diagnosis, *I* didn't want to talk about it. I was embarrassed that I couldn't shake the symptoms on my own. There is a stigma with mental illness that a person who has it is either weak-minded or crazy. In reality, it is an illness—a treatable one.

In the twenty-five years since my first major episode with depression, I have immersed myself in research to understand this illness better so I can live, and help others live, a full life. I've learned a lot from personal experience, books, the Internet, and from talking to people who deal with depression. The following sections contain some of the most important lessons I've learned.

MENTAL VS. PHYSICAL

The label "mental illness" is somewhat of a misnomer. It implies that the illness is all in the head; that the erroneous thinking could be corrected with positive self-talk. Depression does cause erroneous thinking—it distorts perception and reality. But, depression, anxiety and the whole scope of "mental" illnesses are actually *physical* illnesses. They are caused by a chemical imbalance in the body that has mental, emotional, physical, and spiritual manifestations.

This distinction is important because it helps us understand how to treat the illness and recognizes that the illness is just as real as other physical ailments. And, just like with other sicknesses/diseases caused by chemical imbalances (such as diabetes, low thyroid, heart disease, and cancer) the deficit, or surplus, of chemicals needs to be re-balanced.

In depression, these chemicals are most often serotonin and dopamine, but other factors may be involved.

The Pains of Depression

Depression hurts—as in it is *physically* painful—not just emotionally debilitating. This is one of the most misunderstood aspects of mental illness. At its worst, it is an exquisite, acute emotional agony; a burden of sorrow so heavy it can cause a person to hunch over or curl into the fetal position. It is grief, heartache, and disappointment all compounded into one. The pain comes in waves, ebbing and flowing. It can be intense enough to immobilize, or even temporarily paralyze, an individual. Cognitive function becomes impaired because it takes so much mental and emotional energy to cope with the ache.

This description may seem dramatic, but anyone who has experienced the depths of depression will tell you, it is an excruciatingly personal, painful attack of the body, mind, and soul. That's why people who are depressed get a little "crazy." Being in that much pain, or torment, for lack of a better description, over a prolonged period of time makes a person willing to do almost anything to find relief.

There are very few things that can compete with the intense emotional pain of untreated depression, and most of them are harmful or addictive. The most common coping mechanisms are sex, drugs, and alcohol but there are other methods. All of them involve some kind of rush, thrill, or escape—basically, it's a chemical reaction fighting a chemical imbalance.

Chemical Powerhouses

Anti-depressants are powerful drugs—some of the strongest in the industry. They target chemicals in the brain, specifically the serotonin and dopamine mentioned earlier, and are mind-altering and mood stabilizing. Because they are drugs, many people feel drugged while taking them. They have side effects, most of which go away after a few months. They should not be treated casually. They are time sensitive. They should be taken as directed and never stopped suddenly. This will lead to withdrawal both physically and emotionally.

It can be a little challenging to figure out which chemicals are off and by how much as well as discovering which medication is most effective in bringing things back into balance. It may take a combination of drugs, and not just one, to produce desired results. Unlike illnesses such as diabetes and low thyroid, there are no blood tests or other methods of analysis, other than improved mood and behavior, to check if the treatment is correct. Medications are also dispensed in specific doses, which may be too little or too much of a certain chemical. However, with some tweaking and patience, most people are able to find something that works for them.

Anti-depressants build up in the system and eventually stabilize the chemical imbalance. The positive effects can be felt as soon as seven days but may take up to two months to even out. If it's the right medication for you, you should feel it—you will notice a gradual difference in mood and thought processes. The dose may need to be increased for maximum effectiveness, but you will know you're on the right path. If the medications, or dose, are not right, you may have worse symptoms, or show no signs of improvement.

One thing I have found with medications is that, over time, they can lose their effectiveness. Others I've talked to have experienced this as well. I am not sure if this is because the body fights to get back to what it thinks is "normal" or if it builds up a tolerance to the meds. At any rate, be aware this may happen and be open to change.

Even when I found medications that worked, there were still symptoms I had to manage on my own because chemicals fluctuate; environmental triggers fluctuate; life fluctuates.

PERSONAL RESPONSIBILITY & EXPECTATIONS

Just like with other illnesses, there is still a measure of personal responsibility required to deal with the illness from day to day. (See Rebecca's tips in the chapters: Music, The Power of Creation, and Sleep.)

When I was first diagnosed, I wanted to take a pill and forget I had an illness. I thought if I pretended it wasn't that big of a deal, it wouldn't be. I did that for many years yet struggled through all of them. I still functioned in my roles of wife, mother, and other responsibilities, but never felt completely well. It was only when medications began to fail and it took a couple of years to find a combination that worked (years of trying new meds, experiencing the side effects but not the optimal effects, going off meds, experiencing withdrawals, moving on to something new over and over) that I took a more active approach in my medication and overall approach to having depression.

I chose a physician [a nurse practitioner] who had a lot of experience and success treating women with depression. We worked together to create a treatment plan and, with her help, I finally found meds that managed most of my symptoms.

I got counseling. I'd tried a couple of times before but found some therapists used their profession to work through their own issues instead of their clients. So I gave up on it; it is one of my biggest regrets. I really wish I'd pursued it until I found a counselor who fit. It is empowering to have tools to deal with triggers and to discern the difference between reality and distorted perception.

I told people I had depression. I'd always felt the need to keep quiet about my illness, but it became necessary to let people know. When symptoms would flare up, I would be unreliable. I didn't want people to think I was a flake, so I explained what I had and how it affected my ability to function at times. Most people have appreciated understanding my behavior and have not been judgmental about an illness that is just beginning to be openly talked about. That has been empowering too.

I had to adjust my expectations. Depression creates limits on what I can and can't do without becoming overwhelmed. Recognizing that has helped me have more realistic expectations. However, I haven't let depression hold me back from any of the things I really want to do. When I prioritize my time, take care of myself, and do all I can to be healthy, I maximize the ability I do have.

The most important lesson: Just because I have depression doesn't mean I have to be depressed. Depression is an illness; attitude is a choice.

A FINAL THOUGHT

When speaking with others suffering with depression, I have often heard people describe the emotional torment associated with it as "a living hell." I agree that it is. But, in my understanding, Hell is a place for people who have done something really wrong, a punishment for breaking God's commandments. So the association of Hell with depression troubles me. Depressed people typically have done nothing to deserve the troubling feelings of worthlessness *with the exception* of those who use abuse and aggression as a way to cope with depression.

I prefer to think of depression as a type of Gethsemane. Not that any of us would equate ourselves with Jesus Christ, but He took on Himself sorrows that weren't his own and was completely weighed down by them. He prayed for the bitter cup to pass, but it didn't; He had to "drink" it and go on.

Depression, although spiritual in nature, is not something that can be prayed away. It helps, but does not resolve the real issues of physical illness. And, even when that illness is treated, there are still moments that seem like a bitter cup. We have to drink it and keep pressing on.

We are not responsible for having depression, but we are responsible for what we do with it, how we treat it, and how we live with it. Proper medical treatment, personal care, and enhancing the day-to-day environment enables people with emotional illness to live full and productive lives.

PRESS ON.

RISE.

About the Author: Rebecca Clayson is a wife, mother, aspiring author, prolific reader, Snoopy groupie, and chocolate connoisseur. You can read her thoughts about life on her blog 'Observation Beck' at rebeccajclayson.blogspot.com

CHAPTER 29:
The Sunshine Alphabet

by Jeni Farner

I've never seen a doctor for depression, never been diagnosed with an actual condition, and never had breakdowns that conquered all of my abilities; yet I have experienced my share and learned how to keep it at bay. For me, the word *uplift* is the opposite of depression, and it's what we all need to defy the negative life-sucking beast that wants to overtake us.

In understanding how to avoid depression, first thing is to identify our triggers. Mine are not always the same. For example, when I was a teenager, the trigger was severe loneliness and lack of control of my world. Now it's almost the exact opposite: feeling overwhelmed and inadequate as my responsibilities keep mounting.

Why do I feel overwhelmed, why was I lonely, and why did I feel out of control? I'm not going to spend time talking about the "why" reasons because they're mostly irrelevant. Each person has a personal set of problems that can invite depression, but the outcome is ALWAYS negative.

The following are what I call the *ABC's of Depression*. It's a lighthearted way to describe a heavy subject matter.

A - Anguish, Anxiety

B - Blue

C - Cheerless

D - Dark, Desperate, Dread

E - Empty, Exhausted

F - Fearful

G - Gloomy

H - Heartsick, Hollow

I - Imbalanced

J - Jaded

K - Knotted

L - Lost, Lonely

M - Melancholy, Miserable

N - Negative, Numb

O - Overwhelmed, Obsessive

P - Pained

Q - Quiet, Quit

R - Regretful, Restless

S - Sad, Sinking, Spiritless, &

Suicidal

T - Troubled, Tormented

U - Unsatisfied, Unhealthy, & Ugly

V - Vulnerable, Void

W - Weary

X - Xenophobic

Y - Yearning

Z - Zapped

Any of these words hit home to you? I know I can relate to many of the above ABCs.

What does depression look like in my life? Well, I'm tremendously **exhausted**, I have **zero motivation**, and the traffic in my head is directed by negative, negative, **negative thoughts**.

Among the synonyms for **exhaustion** are weariness and depletion. It's much more than being physically tired. It's mental, spiritual, and emotional too. My brain "hurts"—I don't want to think about anything. My spirit is numb. I have no tears to cry—I do NOT want to deal with my feelings, which makes me constantly long for the only non-addictive escape I have, and that's sleep. Well, maybe it is addictive. All I know is I don't want to get out of bed and face anything. The basic daily tasks become heavy clouds hanging over my head.

As for having **no motivation**—I hop on the "just survive" train. I put no extra effort into anything. I do what is absolutely necessary and throw the rest out the window. I find myself ignoring the hard things that I'm confronted with and I let fear take control. Sound familiar?

Fear takes form in a lot of ways, but for me I'm especially prone to constant harping. When I attack my loved ones, I am simultaneously nagging at myself, leaving crushing notes throughout the mental hallways of my brain, AKA—**negative self-talk**.

Oh, this is really depression's star player! It wipes out self-esteem.

The more I feel rejected and defeated, the more hopeless I become. And this takes place by allowing the coach in my head to speak unkindly. It starts with "you idiot, that was so stupid" and can end with "you're ugly and worthless, nobody really cares about you."

I've learned negative self-talk takes over like a wild fire. Once I give heed to unkind thoughts, they can quickly turn into relentless attacks that are hard to stop.

So, I've briefly identified some triggers and how they play out in my life—now what? What have I done and what am I doing to combat depression? Here are my best bits of advice.

Change your belief system: Positive self-talk

This is a BIG one for me. It first starts with recognizing how you talk to yourself in your mind. You have to consciously pay attention.

When I was in my early twenties, I moved in with my normal, loving, wonderful grandparents, who thought I was something special. Their influence on me over the next three years helped change my belief system. They had bookshelves with endless pages on the subjects of self-help, spirituality, energy, healing, and self-improvement. Their modest home was filled with beautiful music and meditative recordings. I spent many hours outdoors maintaining their acre of land—a small forest of trees, flowers, and happy birds. This was the perfect environment for me to heal my inner wounds by learning to listen to myself, love myself, and be kind to me. I would highly suggest finding some books on the previously mentioned subjects. Find a place of peace to meditate and think. It could be your backyard, a chapel, a park, or a quiet art gallery.

I am a lover of scripture and books of spiritual nature. They really helped me get in tune with my inner self. And there's nothing better than feeling impelled to change and overcome. My favorite motivating authors are Louise Hay and Sue Patton Theole. They have great ideas and wonderful affirmations you can practice.

An affirmation is positive self-talk. So when I caught myself saying, "you're a terrible person," I would quickly rebuttal it with, "I am a

GOOD person." This is the affirmation I used over and over and over until it replaced the negative one. This really was the key for my changing. I had a head full of negativity. I think I believed I was a good person deep down inside, but a part of me locked that up and threw away the key. I didn't know how to unlock it until I started reading those books.

I love to write affirmations on my bathroom mirror and hang positive quotes in my closet (someplace where I see it regularly). My friend's therapist told her to hang pictures of Christ all over her house. You could do this with any person who fills your mind with peace. The idea is to cancel out those awful thoughts and replace them with kind ones. I have my grandmother's beautiful face on my wall.

Control the things you can: Reduce your load

Live life one day at a time, or even one minute at a time if you have to. I get overwhelmed easily by thinking of all the tasks waiting for me. I like to write a to-do list, reread it a couple times, then cross off the things that really don't matter. A good way to know if it matters is to ask yourself if it is something that will lift you up, make you better (or the person you're doing it for). Do I really need to sign my kids up for baseball and soccer and piano this season? Oh my gosh—pick ONE!! Why do we feel pressure to do everything? Does it matter if I hand-make my thank you cards, shop at three different stores for the best bargain, or reply to all my comments on Facebook?

Some sacrifices are necessary and some are not. Simplify as much as possible so you have the energy and time available for the complicated, necessary things that life is full of. Things like fighting an illness, nurturing a newborn, tackling the mountain of bills, and mowing the lawn (okay—that one isn't complicated, but if your yard is as big as mine, it's very time consuming).

Take care of yourself

I know, I know—no motivation is a common result of depression. So what will magically help you want to take care of yourself? Starting on the previous steps should help you feel motivated enough to make subtle changes. Here's some ideas:

- Get your hair done (in a manageable low maintenance style).
- Paint your toes.
- Put a single daisy or sunflower in a vase on your bathroom counter. (My bathroom is a great place to put motivational items because initially I look at myself in the mirror and don't like what I see. A flower or quote generates a good feeling in me, so it makes it easier to think positively about myself.)
- Have a root beer float or buy a box of chocolates or a green smoothie, if that's what you really like!
- Leave the dirty dishes and read a book instead.

Gordon B. Hinckley said it best when he wrote, "Life is meant to be enjoyed, not just endured," This is in big print in my home. I have a special needs boy who has an irreversible heart disease. He requires much of my time and most of my energy. Life as a caregiver has certainly seen its fair share of the joyless and mundane. I desperately need Hinckley's reminder to find the joy—because it's there!

As human beings, we all experience the grasp of depression in one form or another, and it never stops trying to control our thoughts, our countenance, and our outlook on life. It's a constant battle that we must fight. Find the little things that make you smile and hang on to them; for me it is the *Sunshine Alphabet*.

Read the author's full story: https://www.lds.org/ensign/2016/02/depression?lang=eng

The Sunshine Alphabet
by Jeni Farner

A - Awesome
B - Beautiful, Brave, Believe
C - Courage
D - Delight
E - Extraordinary, Endure, Energy
F - Fearless
G - Good, Gratitude
H - Healthy, Happy, Hope
I - Immovable
J - Joy
K - Kind, Knowledgeable
L - Love, Light
M - Mighty, Meaningful
N - New
O - Okay
P - Peace, Praiseworthy
Q - Quality
R - Rested
S - Satisfied, Safe, Strong
T - Teachable, Trust
U - Unyielding, Useful
V - Valid, Valuable
W - Wise, Wonderful
X - Xenial
Y - Yes!
Z - Zest

Press On.

Rise.

About the Author: **Jeni Farner** is a writer for Grace Lane Authors. Read more of her experiences at gracelaneauthors.com.

CHAPTER 30:
Tools Of Triumph

by Camille Ballou

I'm sitting in the Wal-Mart parking lot on my lunch break. The engine is idling, the radio playing some worn out hit from some no-talent pop star. People come and go, carrying on with their lives. They smile and laugh, emotions playing across their faces.

But I don't notice any of that. My mind is a fog, and I am staring at nothing, too numb to even cry at this point. I suck in a deep breath and blow it out.

I want to die.

And all I can focus on is which method I would have the guts to follow through with. Pills? Asphyxiation? Jumping off a bridge into oncoming traffic? A gun? A knife?

Half of these things I don't have access to and the other half scare me too much.

I curse.

I think of my husband. Of my two little girls. And I think of what a coward I am. With a shaking hand, I pick up my cell phone and call my sister, too ashamed to call my husband.

"Help," is all I need to say, and she takes the burden out of my hands. She makes phone calls and coordinates arrangements, and by that evening, I am in the car with my husband driving to the E.R. in downtown Salt Lake City.

"Why are you here?" the registrar asks me.

"I'm afraid I'm going to hurt myself."

"I see. And do you have insurance?'

"Yes."

Next is the nurse.

"Why are you here?"

"I'm afraid I'm going to hurt myself."

"I see."

Then the doctor.

"Why are you here?"

"I'm afraid I'm going to hurt myself."

"I see."

They see. Do they really? Do they truly see?

No, I'm just another patient to turn through the queue that night. Man with a broken foot in Room 3. Child needing stitches in Room 1. Suicidal crazy lady in Room 2. Check. Check. Check.

I am discharged from the Emergency Room with admittance instructions to the hospital across the valley that has an open bed in their psychiatric ward. I have to go home and pack a bag according to the instructions—no shoelaces, drawstrings, sharp objects—you know, things you can manage to hang or stab yourself with.

The forty-five minute drive across town is eternal. My husband and I are both terrified, full of emotions we can't put words to. When we arrive, he comes upstairs with me to the fifth floor for admittance.

The night nurse that greets us asks me, "Do you understand that, although you are self-admitting, you will be unable to leave according to your own free will? You will be here, in lockdown, until released by the doctor. Do you understand?"

I nod yes. I see.

But like the nurses and doctors in the Emergency Room, I really don't see. I am oblivious to what is in store for mi. sign the admittance papers and my husband hands me my bag, hugs me, and walks away.

As the door closes and locks behind him and I am utterly alone . . . as they search my bag and take away some of my belongings . . . as they march me, barefoot, down the cold, empty, dark hallway to my room, anxiety overtakes me, and all the numbness I felt crumbles away as I realize the weight of the situation I am in.

I crawl onto the bed, fully clothed, and finally let myself cry until I fall asleep sometime in the middle of the night.

THE THIEF

Depression is a thief.

It steals a person's drive, self-confidence, clarity and joy.

For as long as I can remember, I have been depressed. Perhaps in varying degrees, depending on my life circumstances, but always depressed. It is a word that became synonymous with my very name. It was my identity.

When I admitted myself to the psych ward, the word depression wasn't strong enough to describe me or what I was feeling any longer because it was so much more. So much more than a mere feeling of sadness or hopelessness. It was all consuming.

I was at the lowest point of my life, and I realized I had two choices: I could learn to cope and save myself, my marriage and my family, or I could give up, succumb and let the rats of mental illness pick me apart until there was nothing left.

Some may think the choice would be clear. Simple.

But I assure you it was not. The choice to change requires hard work and discipline. The choice to give in to the cancer of depression, although logically not the right choice, is the easier choice.

And easy is always enticing.

But somewhere in the recesses of my mind, in the corner of my cold, lifeless heart, was a spark. A spark of life that was burning, not only for my husband and kids, but also for me.

And so I made my choice.

I took my first Prozac when I was thirteen.

Since then I have been on Lexapro, Zoloft, Pristiq, Effexor, Wellbutrin, Abilify, Xanax, Klonopin, and a few others I can't even remember or pronounce in various doses and combinations.

The thing with medications, though? They can only do so much. Taking pills for depression and having it fix you is like an obese person popping a diet pill and then chasing it with a cheeseburger combo meal. If I learned anything during the three days I spent in the psych ward, it was that pills are only as good as the effort you put in.

They are tools, not crutches.

And if someone is to build something using tools, a life, for instance, they need more than one tool to do it.

A house cannot be built with a single hammer. Nor can a house be built by merely wishing it were so.

Become aware

The best offense is a good defense in most cases.

Not where depression is concerned. Putting up your defenses is the quickest way to shut down and self-implode. The first thing I had to learn was to recognize why I was doing certain things. Why was I lashing out at my children? Why was I lying in bed staring at nothing? Why was I binging? Why was I withdrawing from my husband?

It is not easy to understand your motivations. But each time I found myself in a situation where I was questioning why, I tried to come up with an answer.

Why was I angry with my children? Because they were making messes in the house and a dirty house gave me anxiety. Why was I binging? Because I wanted to feel full, soothed instead of empty inside. Why was I withdrawing? Because I felt guilty.

And on it went. I analyzed my actions, my negative thoughts, and my words so I could understand why.

It didn't mean I had to do anything about it at that point; I just needed to become aware. I needed to add voice to my feelings.

This helped not only me, but my husband as well. He was able to better help and support me when I could answer his question of "What is wrong?" with something other than "Nothing" or "I don't know."

Therapy

I had tried therapy multiple times in the seventeen years leading up to my hospitalization, but I never took it seriously because I always assumed they didn't understand and they didn't know what they were talking about. For some reason, I thought I was an exception to the little boxes they put their patients in. When I was released, I was required to follow up with a psychiatrist and a therapist. I made a choice this time around to conduct an experiment: I was going to follow every instruction, every piece of advice I was given by my therapist to see if it would work. To see if maybe, just maybe, they knew something more than I did.

I spent the next seven years doing everything my counselors asked me to do.

Sometimes I was asked to do little things—like get out of bed, take a shower. Sometimes I was asked to do big things—like learn to forgive and love myself.

Eventually the little things built upon themselves and made big differences. Eventually my thinking errors resolved themselves. Eventually my depression went into remission.

What I realized through this was that, even though the professional advice was valuable, the more important factor was having someone to talk to. Someone to help me sort out my feelings and confused thoughts.

I was lucky enough to have good mental health benefits associated with my health insurance. I was lucky enough to find a therapist that fit my schedule, with whom I could make and keep regular appointments because it didn't interfere with my job or home responsibilities.

I was certainly lucky.

But that doesn't mean that a trusted friend or family member can't serve the same purpose as a therapist, if carefully chosen. It must be someone who will listen and not insert their own agenda. It must be someone whose opinion you respect. It must be someone who can gently make suggestions without causing your defenses to rise. It must be someone who can dedicate time to listen on a consistent basis. If you wait until you need to talk to someone, it's probably too late. Talking when you are in a more rational headspace goes further than when you are not.

Me-Time

Realize and accept that it is okay to take time during the day or the week for you. Life is demanding. It always will be, no matter your circumstances. I found that it was much easier to serve and nurture my children, to perform well at my job, to get out of bed and clean the house, to cook a meal, or whatever else life wanted from me at the time if I had taken some me-time.

And let me be clear: lying in bed and moping is not considered me-time. Me time has to be something that nurtures your soul.

For me it was reading a good book, getting my hair done, polishing my toes, or going on a date with my husband. Later, as I became healthier, it involved taking time each day to go to the gym or run a few miles.

Me-time shouldn't be expensive. While there will be times you may splurge, I'm not suggesting weekly spa visits or shopping sprees. I am suggesting doing something simple that will fill your emotional cup, if only a little at a time. As I mentioned before, depression is a thief, and if you don't take time to stockpile your reserves, it will bleed you dry.

Develop Hobbies

I will never forget the arts and crafts time in the hospital. I thought it was stupid—a room full of psych ward patients being forced to make beaded bracelets and necklaces. I remember picking out the letters to spell each of my kid's names. I remember creating a pattern with the colors to fill in the spaces between the letters. I remember stringing the beads together and creating something I could give my children when I finally got to go home.

Most of all, I remember my mind being distracted for that hour block of time and forgetting that I was depressed, forgetting to feel sorry for myself.

Working with my hands became better than any therapy or pill I had ever taken, and I knew I needed to find an outlet, a hobby, to occupy my mind for a little while each day. I had cross-stitched as a child, so when I was released from the hospital, I decided that would be a good craft to pick up again, since I already knew how and enjoyed it somewhat. I went to the store and picked out several pattern books, threads, and various canvases to stitch on—pillows, towels, and fabric that could be framed eventually. That Christmas I made kitschy holiday towels for everyone in my family. The year after, I made and framed a beautiful artistic piece for my mother-in-law. I made pillows for others in the family.

It was a hobby I could do in front of the TV or lying in bed, so it spoke to the depressed person in me who still wanted to lie around all day. I just added one important component to my lying-around time—I occupied my mind and hands so my depression could be placed on the shelf while I worked. On top of the relief I got from my depressive thoughts, I found joy in making and giving things to others.

Believe in a Higher Power

Some believe in a God; some don't. The truth I have found is that at some point, a depressed person has to come to the realization that they themselves are powerless to overcome their illness on their own.

A depressed or mentally ill person is no more at fault for their situation than someone with a non-lifestyle related cancer or Type

1 Diabetes. At some point the guilt and the burden of your illness has to be turned over to a Higher Power.

You have to let it go. But how?

For some that means prayer to a God of their choosing. For some that means meditation.

I am not suggesting that prayer and meditation will fix everything, because it won't. Believe me.

What I am suggesting is that through prayer and meditation you can let go of the guilt you are harboring, you can take the burden from your shoulders and send it out to the cosmos. And you can believe that your Higher Power will offer support and sustain you as you work through your healing process.

You are not alone.

Even though you may feel that way, and you may be alone based on your circumstance in this life, believing in a Higher Power means that you are not.

You have a partner, a confidant, a friend.

Have a Cause

A cause is something that gives rise to an action. This definition doesn't specify the magnitude of the cause, just that it results in an action. The magnitude can increase over time, as you heal you find yourself capable of a little bit more, and a little bit more.

> Today I will take a shower.
>
> Today I will cook a meal.
>
> Today I will take a shower and cook a meal.
>
> Today I will take a shower, cook a meal, and do the dishes.

Until eventually…

> Today I will go for a walk.
>
> Today I will visit a friend.
>
> Today I will play with my kids.

Your cause can also be bigger and extend beyond today, once you are ready.

I want to finish school.

I want to get a new job.

I want to improve my relationships.

I want to serve in my community.

I always had a cause for the day, a cause for the week, and a long-term cause. I am a goal-oriented person. I like checking things off a list. I like feeling accomplished, and having a cause provided a focus for me. It allows me to set goals with myself and feel proud when I achieve them.

Depression typically leads people to become self-centered through necessity. It is all you can do to make it through the day sometimes—worrying about me, me, me. Your cause can be focused on you, as long as it has a productive result of some kind—like taking a shower. You aren't trying to save the world here; you are just trying to save yourself.

Exercise and Healthy Eating

I know, I know. Tell me to shut up right now. No one wants to hear this one. I won't get on my soapbox, though, because I am one of the worst offenders of this tool.

I will only tell you that as a compulsive, binge-eater who has fluctuated weight like a yo-yo over the last twenty-five years and has tried practically every diet known to man, I have some experience in this arena and can personally attest to the impact of exercise and healthy eating.

When I eat high-fat, high-calorie, high-carbohydrate foods, I feel foggy and lethargic. When I eat proteins, fruits and vegetables and complex carbohydrates, I can think more clearly. Knowing this fact, however, doesn't always make my food choices simple. Sometimes I simply don't care. But the fact remains that what I feed my body does have an impact on the way I feel and my mental state. When I am ready to make a change, one of the first things I try to change is my eating habits.

In addition to food, exercise of some kind is important. I had heard people speak of the benefits of endorphins, but it wasn't until I was challenged to run a half marathon with my sister and began training that I understood. I became a runner, slow and steady, but a runner at heart. I ran five half marathons between 2012 and 2014. During that time, my depression was in complete remission. After my last race in 2014, my life circumstances changed somewhat, I let my eating habits revert to the old ways, and I stopped running. I don't think it's a coincidence that over the next year, the depression crept back in.

Patience, Persistence and Perseverance

None of these tools are easy. None of them alone are magical solutions. And nothing lasting changes overnight. But piece by piece, things start to fit together. The small things build and compound until they are big things. The things I learned to help me cope, to help me overcome, would have been useless had I not done one thing that night in the hospital: made the choice. By making that choice, I became the carpenter, the brick mason, the contractor that put the tools into action to build my life. Without that choice, the tools would have laid lifeless at my feet. Without that choice, that conviction and determination, I would have given up. I would have taken the easy way out when things were hard. I would never have known it was possible for me to not be depressed. And I would never have known how sweet it is when the darkness clears.

Be patient. Be persistent.

Choose you.

PRESS ON.

RISE.

About the Author: Camille Ballou works as a CPA, spends her free time volunteering for the local FFA chapter, and hangs out with her family and their beloved Labrador.

CHAPTER 31:

Not Beaten

by Janet Bernice

I have worked with my brain gifts, for that is what I call depression combined with ADHD, since 1991, over twenty years. There are specific things I do and don't do. In the long run, depression, in particular, has strengthened me and given me tremendous empathy for others, along with a desire to not be beaten by a physical ailment I have.

In 1991, I was in weekly therapy for many reasons, many of which wouldn't get me on a talk show today, but enough to deplete my adrenal system and to bring on a serious fight with daily, often debilitating, depression. My therapist said, "You need to face that you have chronic depression, which is why you're not able to put into practice the tools I'm trying to give you."

My first thought was that I needed to be a stronger-willed person and pull myself together. My second thought was I'm less than everyone else and I can't let anyone know I have this problem. I was also a compulsive over-eater, and when depression was at its worst, could sleep away most of the day, waking at four or five p.m. and staying up till three in the morning instead. I had trouble keeping a job because whatever energy I *did* have, I used to take care of my children as a single mother. Children were the reason I was in therapy, anyway; I didn't want to pass on bad habits or make them feel they weren't loved or taken care of. I had to work on me to make sure they had what they needed. My children helped save my life.

I am way down the road past what seemed to be impossible days without end. I have had a successful career helping others and finished a master's degree; all my children are married with children of their own.

What I learned: depression is a pre-disposition in the body caused by a misfire in the brain and then within the system. It has nothing to do with a person's character or worth. Situations can acerbate it, but not cause depression, as it is a real disease. In 1991, when first diagnosed, I began to take an anti-depressant; I still take it. I have learned to avoid caffeinated drinks (I no longer drink sodas) and processed foods, for the most part anyway. I still struggle with sleeping when I'm feeling quite low, but can generally face it down with self-talk: "Are you really tired or do you just need a break? Are you thirsty? Your stomach's full so you don't need anything to eat . . . you can do hard things; you have before, you can do it again."

Positive affirmations also help tremendously, as does being around others who are unconditional in their love and friendship. I am picky about the people I allow into my life, knowing what can trigger emotional difficulties and thus plunge me into a situationally induced depression. Here are some of my favorite affirmations, on my office wall, read often:

"Why fit in when you were born to stand out?" – Dr. Seuss

"I am only one, but still I am one. I cannot do everything, but still I can do something; and because I cannot do everything, I will not refuse to do something that I can do." – Edward Everett Hale

"Fear is a reaction. Courage is a decision." – Winston Churchill

"Your compassion does not include yourself, it is incomplete." – Buddha

"No pessimist ever discovered the secrets of the stars, or sailed to an uncharted land, or opened a new heaven to the horizon of the spirit."
– Helen Keller

"When you're trying to motivate yourself, appreciate the fact that you're even thinking about making a change. And as you move forward, allow yourself to be good enough." – Alice Domar, PhD

"Hold on to what is good, even if it's a handful of earth. Hold on to what you believe, even if it's a tree that stands by itself. Hold on to what you must do, even if it's a long way from here. Hold on to your life, even if it's easier to let go. Hold on to my hand, even if I've gone away from you." — Pueblo Indian Prayer

"Remember, no one can make you feel inferior without your consent." — Eleanor Roosevelt (1884-1962); U.S. First Lady

"Don't ever give up. Don't ever give in. Don't ever stop trying. Don't ever sell out. And if you find yourself succumbing to one of the above for a brief moment, pick yourself up, brush yourself off, whisper a prayer, and start where you left off. But never, ever, ever give up." — Richelle E. Goodrich, Author

"Expect to have hope rekindled. Expect your prayers to be answered in wondrous ways. The dry seasons do not last. The spring rains will come." — Sarah Ban Breathnach, writer

I have taken responsibility for how it is in my life. My body is not perfect and presents me with challenges, many unseen. However using the tools I've learned and practiced through the years gives me hope, helps me to succeed many times when I don't think it possible, and continues to inform daily living. Depression will not go away completely, but it can be managed. Life can become fulfilling and satisfying in spite of depression or, actually, because of it. The strengths developed to manage depression also are a benefit for other areas of life.

PRESS ON.
RISE.

About the Author: Janet M. Bernice, MA, is a writer and an online college instructor.

CHAPTER 32:
The Most Difficult Battle

by Lori Conger

When I was barely eleven years old, my life changed forever. I went to school one day a happy, carefree fifth-grader and came home a traumatized, withdrawn shell of a girl who was suddenly afraid of everything. Our elementary school was taken hostage that day by a madman and his wife, a shopping cart of explosives, and a homemade bomb. We were held captive for two and a half very long hours before the bomb was accidentally detonated and we found ourselves escaping a burning classroom, gun fire, and the thickest, blackest smoke we had ever seen. Life, as precious as it was to us, would never be the same.

Now I am a forty-one-year-old wife and mother of five. It has been thirty years since that fateful day in May. I have grown and changed in many ways. I have graduated from college, fulfilled a full-time mission for my church, worked hard at various endeavors, and given my all to my husband and children; I have fulfilled dreams and worked hard to become the woman I long to become. But the scars from that experience have remained with me. Most people would say I am ambitious, capable, happy and perhaps even inspiring. What they do not know is that on a regular basis I am fighting the most difficult battle of my life: depression associated with Post Traumatic Stress Disorder (PTSD).

The thing about PTSD is that it sneaks up and grabs you around the throat when you least expect it. Life can be moving along just fine. You can feel healthy and happy and capable—even "normal"—and then suddenly you can't cope with even the small details of your life. You feel lonely and scared. Despair starts to settle in and you find yourself wondering how you ever felt free from this monster of depression that threatens to completely overwhelm you and take away everything good in your life, leaving you with nothing but broken fragments of what could have been.

Sometimes I feel strong and in control, completely capable of reaching my divine destiny and becoming the woman I want desperately to become. I feel free; I feel hopeful; I feel happy.

But in a single moment, I feel as small and helpless as a child, curled up in a ball in my closet, hoping to block away the pain of knowing I can never become what I hope to, never really overcome my problems. I feel completely uncertain of what my future—or even tomorrow—holds for me. It is frightening and overwhelming. Dread fills my whole being and threatens to swallow me whole. It is in these moments I feel truly hopeless.

I wonder: *How did I get to this place? Wasn't it just yesterday I was productive and strong, conquering the world, feeling in control? How then can I today be so completely exhausted—mind, body and spirit—so that even breathing in and out feels like a monumental task? Why is my mind foggy and my confidence completely destroyed? How did this happen? And how do I find myself again?*

At these times I know if I do not reach out for Divine help, I will lose myself to despair. And so I pray—no, I *plead*, I *beg* for God's mercy and grace, seeking for the peace only He can give. He rescues me time and time again as a sweet, undeniable calm settles over me, and I am reminded that things will be okay. I am assured that I am not alone in this battle and that light will again shine in the morning. I take deep, deliberate breaths and simply hold on.

It's not like all of my problems immediately vanish; the pain is still there, as raw as ever, threatening to literally destroy me, but I begin to feel even the slightest bit of hope, and I have learned that hope is a life-saving feeling. Hope gets me out of bed day after day. Hope dispels the fear and chases despair away. Hope gives me a reason to not give up, even when I feel it is pointless to keep trying. Hope allows me a moment to catch my breath and keep fighting, even though I know the war is long and the battles excruciatingly difficult.

Hope is almost always followed by peace. To me, peace is the most wonderful feeling in the world! It trumps the more powerful emotions like excitement and anger and even joy because it is real and it is all encompassing. Peace has a power all its own: the power to calm fears, to clear minds, to replenish souls. Peace is a gift from heaven and is worth every effort to obtain. It is the calm assurance that God is on our side, and therefore we can and will conquer the enemy of depression and the aftermath of PTSD.

It is no secret that without my faith, my life would be very different. Perhaps I would not even still be here. I cannot say for sure, but what I can say for sure is that God's love is real, and it is the most powerful thing on earth. No matter how difficult our circumstances or how dark the night, God's love never changes. It is there like a beacon of light to fill our empty souls and make us realize our lives have value, that our worth never changes and that with His help, we can overcome.

I know the battle I am facing, this battle of PTSD and depression, cannot be conquered on my own. I do not have the strength to do it. But I also know that with the help of God, I can. I can make it through the difficult stretches, one day at a time, until I am back on my feet and able to cope again. I can have more days of thriving rather than just surviving. I can feel whole once again if I simply hold onto Him and all He offers me.

I have found prayer to be the most powerful weapon of defense in the midst of my struggles. In my experience, there is nothing that brings such immediate relief and freshens perspective quite like wrestling with my Maker in mighty prayer, cleaving unto Him who has the power and desire to lift me up again above the gulf of inadequacy, loneliness, failure and despair, and remind me of all I have to offer the world and all I have to live for. And so, I reach out to Him, the Prince of Peace, and give everything over to the One who can make me feel whole again.

Although it is difficult to begin, therapy can be another tool to help fight the effects of depression. Sometimes we need a listening ear from someone who is not part of our daily lives. We need to be able to unashamedly share our struggles and bear a bit of our souls to someone who understands better what we are experiencing and can offer help without judgment. I have been extremely grateful for the psychologists who at different periods of my life have helped me pick up the pieces and see things clearly again. They have provided me with tools to more effectively prevent the onslaught of depressive patterns of behavior and fight the battles I face. They remind me I am not broken, and to someone like me who so often feels useless and disjointed, that is a wonderful truth to cling to!

I have learned to love harder when I feel the most angst in my soul. I wrap my tired arms around my children and my husband many times each day; I whisper my love to them and hold them a little longer than normal; I remind them how good they are and how important they are in my life. I do this because I do in fact love them with all my heart, but I also do it because I yearn for that love and warmth to be reciprocated back to me, to fill my soul with belonging and stability. It is a wonderful thing to love and be loved! If only my family could understand how much their unconditional love fills my soul to bursting and gives me the courage to keep putting one foot in front of the other and to never, ever quit! They are my biggest reason for persevering. I love them far too much to ever let them down. I know they too will face difficult challenges in life, and I long for them to never give up, to forge ahead with faith and courage and determination, and so I must too. How grateful I am for the incentive they give me to do my best, even when sometimes that means little more than getting up in the morning and slowly plodding onward.

Music has become a powerful tool in restoring peace and calming fears. When I feel I cannot bear the chaos, pressure, and demands of life, I retreat to my bedroom, shut the door, and lie down next to beautiful piano renditions of the sacred hymns. I close my eyes and try to lose myself to the hopeful messages in the inspired lyrics, allowing the beautiful strains of the piano to wash over me and calm all the emotions threatening to destroy me. Strength begins to flow into me as I silently focus on words such as, "Fear not, I am with thee; oh, be not dismayed/ For I am thy God and will still give thee aid/ I'll strengthen thee, help thee, and cause thee to stand/ Upheld my righteous, omnipotent hand" and "Be still my soul; the Lord is on thy side." The music calms my troubled heart and gives me the courage to get back up and keep trying.

Sometimes I wonder what the future really holds for me, a woman who longs to be a light to others, to raise a righteous family and to use her gifts and abilities to make a difference in the world, and yet who is so often debilitated by the traumatizing effects of PTSD. I don't have the answer to that question and to the others that plague my mind so often.

But I do know that I am not alone.

And that makes all the difference.

Life will always hold its share of challenges, especially for those of us who suffer from PTSD and/or depression, but there is always hope. We have not been left to fight the enemy alone; the Lord is with us. He loves us with a love we cannot understand, and He will always be there to rescue us. He has even promised angels to bear us up and strengthen us in our most difficult moments, and He always keeps his promises. If we trust in Him, turn to Him, and give our struggles to Him, we will find the hope we long for and we will be whole again, even if just for a while. In the end, He will make up the difference. And so I cleave to Him; I take one day at a time; and I never give up hope!

PRESS ON.
RISE.

About the Author: Lori Conger is a mother, wife, speaker and survivor of the Cokeville Elementary hostage crisis. Learn more at www.loriconger.blogspot.com.

CHAPTER 33:

Paralysis to Progress

by Nathan and Heather Ogden
with Jodi Orgill Brown

Special Note About the Authors, Nathan and Heather Ogden:

As an active young husband and father, Nathan Ogden suffered a devastating neck break from a ski accident, leaving him paralyzed from the waist down. His wife became his caregiver and biggest advocate, and together they determined to move forward and conquer life. Their attitudes and survival were further tested when Nathan fell off a hospital X-ray table, erasing his progress and leaving him a highly-impaired quadriplegic. Years after learning to navigate their changed life, Heather suffered a traumatic brain injury after their car was hit by a drunk driver. Yet together, the Ogdens do not let anything paralyze them from progress. Nathan's book, *Unfrozen*, teaches how to conquer the excuses and lies we tell ourselves and enable us to discover our true potential. Find them online at: www.nathanogden.com

UNFROZEN—NATHAN'S STORY

"Bring it on," were the first three words I uttered after my wife told me my neck was broken—for the second time.

Heather said a bout with pneumonia had literally knocked me out—and I wouldn't wake up. She called an ambulance and they transported me to the hospital, but while I was unconscious in the E.R., I fell off an X-ray table and broke my neck.

The break from the fall was higher in my neck, at the C6 level. That meant I lost the use of my hands, triceps, and all of the progress I'd made during the year's recovery since my first break.

Still, better that it happened to me twice than just once to someone else. By the second break, we knew what we were doing; we knew how to make progress and accomplish the small goals toward movement.

"I am still going to walk again. This setback will not alter *that* goal," I promised both of us.

STALLED

Weeks later, the pale white-washed wall stared me in the face. Unable to move or turn my head, I had no choice but to stare back. Even a spider would have been welcome; anything to tell me there was life outside the space that trapped my mind and body. The world may as well have been ten feet wide, because that was the extent of my sheet-rocked tomb.

The screws that drilled into my head were part of a contraption called a halo. Ironic. A more fitting name would have been an iron mask, for it made me feel both trapped and invisible. Though I knew the torturing device served a purpose, no angelic freedoms came with my halo, only frustration. How I longed to lay my head down and feel the soft coolness of a pillow against my cheek.

"*Arghhhh!*" I sounded my best pirate yell, but the frustration just bounced off the wall and hit me in the face.

The abilities I'd worked so hard to revive after the first break were gone—along with the optimism I'd felt after the break. A new sensation rooted in the pit of my stomach, and as much as I didn't want to admit it, I knew something had changed.

It isn't coming back this time.

No matter how I tried to fade into the sleep of medication, reality always jerked me awake and forced me to reevaluate everything.

What do I do now? Am I strong enough to keep pushing forward?

Superman, or at least Christopher Reeves, his actor counterpart, was paralyzed, but all the pictures showed him appearing content, hopeful, and smiling for the camera. I tried to keep smiling, to assure everyone that I would save the world, but my enemy battled me on the inside.

Mentally I fought seemingly endless struggles for my future. Again and again I tried to defeat the foes in my head, but a single thought prevented me from victory.

I will be in this wheelchair for the rest of my life.

STEALING TRUTH

Negativity spun in my head like a carnival ride. Even when I managed to work my way out of one set of thoughts, another would work its way in. *What can I do? Am I smart enough to do things with my mind because I can't do them physically?* I wasn't sure I would be able to get off the stupid ride, or if I did, if I would like who I'd be when I got out.

The hardest part for me was not just that my dreams disappeared, but that I took dreams from others. My wife would never have a husband who could take her swimming below a cascading waterfall in Hawaii, and my son would never go fishing at a lake in the mountains with his dad. I stole their experiences, and all I got was guilt and physical agony.

Guilt rarely takes a work break. I tortured myself thinking about how my kids would never have a dad who could jump and cheer on the field or coach their soccer games. Why even bother going? So I talked myself out of going—and then always regretted it. I hate that guilt and regret tag team against us and put negative scenarios in our minds, but I find those two devils do work together.

The internal feelings and doubts often matched my physical pain. Most people assume that paralysis means you can't feel anything. The truth is quite the opposite. I can't control my limbs and body parts, nor feel some external wounds, but I am constantly zapped by stinging nerves that fire in my body. I've heard that amputees continue to experience pain after the loss of a limb—and I've wondered if it is something similar, an eerie reminder of what you don't have.

I didn't live with a constant state of depression, but for a while, the visits occurred with mounting frequency. Depression became the unwanted guest in our home; I tried to keep going as though he wasn't upsetting our routine and invading our personal lives, but the truth didn't have a closet to hide in.

After every visit, it became harder to ask the guest to leave. Depression settled in, and at one point, I no longer noticed he was there; he just became part of the background of my life. And that was the problem.

TURNING POINTS

At times I saw the mess that Depression left in my life. Then I would think, "Something has to change." But, there was no epiphany that ever made it happen. Rather, there were many moments, many attempts, and just as many failures. I tried, but I just couldn't get traction. I made promises to evict the negativity and to make room for positivity. But the confrontations never happened.

Then came the day when my wife mentioned the D word: *Divorce*. The woman who'd promised to be with me forever said if I didn't change something, she would, and that would mean losing her. I knew she loved me; she was one of the few who still treated me like I still had something to offer the world. So many others just pretended I was invisible, but Heather always saw me. But I had broken her trust—I had promised her time and again that I would try, *just try*, to help myself, and I hadn't kept my promises.

Over the next few days, the *D* word roared like a freight train in my mind. The horn of self-doubt blared louder than ever before. I didn't know how serious she was, but the blindside effect forced me to reevaluate my behavior in hopes I would still have a future with my wife.

I began to realize I was letting the unwanted guest push my wife—and my life—away from me.

At the time, I was taking nerve pain medication, which also acted as an antidepressant. Family members told me that when I was on it, I wasn't myself; I was just kind of *there*, part of the background.

Sometime in the hazy days that followed, I made a decision that if I was going to live life, if I was going to fight each day to survive, then I wanted to be me. Unwanted guests were no longer welcome. That meant I had to make a difficult exchange: Get off the medication, but deal with more pain.

I wanted to live without the mess that Depression left in its wake. But most of all, I just wanted to be ME again so I could keep the girl I love.

NOT A SUPERHERO

Getting off my medication was not pretty. Mount Everest-sized emotional swings made me cry during coffee commercials and laugh uncontrollably at inappropriate times. I wondered if it was worth it (and always decided it was) and wondered if I could really do it (and some days are still better than others). It was not, and I was not, perfect. But in time, things got better, though nerve pain still tries to cripple my resolve.

One of the most meaningful lessons I learned is that there is no Superman. When you meet someone with impeccable hair, an amazing job, a beautiful wife and family who is able to fly, looks good in tights, and seems perfect in every way, they are not real. Everyone, and I mean everyone, has their own Kryptonite that weakens the power to fight. Depression is a very real Kryptonite, but is also a very treatable condition.

THE PARAMETERS OF FORWARD

With the medication out of my system and my determination back in, I decided I needed to do something different; to set some parameters for my life:

- Faith first. I won't watch TV, surf Internet, or use social media until I read the Holy Scriptures.
- Self-Care. I will eat breakfast before I go into my (home) office.
- Serve. I will serve someone in someway each day.
- Exercise. Even if I can only push myself for one lap around the house, I will do some form of exercise.

At the end of the day, I may wish I'd done more, but I'd also know

I did something I could feel good about.

Small practices, when practiced consistently, form the building blocks of change. These little steps were the start of my turnaround.

DECISION POINTS

I still don't always make the right decision. But when I have a choice to make, when my ten-year old is out playing basketball by herself, I have the choice to participate, even though it is not how I'd want to.

The effort of *doing* weighs a lot less than the regret and guilt of looking back and wishing you could change it. "I should have" is the worst phrase in life. It means you are not living your life the way you want to live it.

When you make a decision, you have to distinguish—do I have faith or do I have fear? Sometimes it may be faith in the possibility for a better life, or faith in passion, or faith in purpose. Act on that faith no matter how hard it is. When you act, you can have peace; peace that you've done right by yourself. Peace and regret can't live together. Acting on your faith doesn't guarantee perfect outcomes, but it means you will live with peace instead of regret.

CLIMBING OUT

Climbing out of depression or hardship is not one simple task or straightforward path, but the following six methods empowered me to take my life back.

Communication. Communicate with others, and most importantly, with yourself. It's tough to accept the fact that you're suffering from depression or anxiety, and it is hard to invest the time and energy to treat it. But before you can begin to get help, you must admit to yourself and others that depression, YOUR depression, is real. That was hard for me to do. Admitting I was mired in depression was as hard as coming to grips with paralysis.

Set an end date. Nobody wants to feel like they don't have control, and that's exactly what depression will do. But you know what, it's okay to want to hide from the world. The important thing is not to let it control you.

If you want to sit on the couch all day or wallow in your bed, go for it. It's all right to take a time out, just *give yourself a time limit*. After one movie, one day, or one week, you must say to yourself, this experience has been difficult, but I'm over it. Then it's time to do something productive that will improve your mood. For me, this meant trying to do something that would help someone else, from reading to my kids to (attempting to) help my wife.

Make a decision. It can be difficult to climb out of the hole that you're in when you have no motivation or direction. That's why it's so critical to just make a decision. Any decision! It doesn't matter how big or small, but I recommend starting small. When you're not making some kind of progress, you'll never gain the confidence needed to change and succeed. Just the act of making a decision helps reduce worry and anxiety. During my initial climb out of depression, that meant choosing to have a conversation with my kids, or even eat a meal, rather than to just sit in a solitary sulk. Make a decision to get out of bed and take a shower. Then build upon that positive emotion and choose to do something else. One little mind trick I learned was to count down from five to one (instead of counting up). We are taught that in life, a countdown means prepare for LAUNCH.

Service. The National Science Foundation says we have between 12,000 and 50,000 thoughts each day, and therapist Norman Wright estimates 75% of them are negative. Serving those around you will be one of your greatest tools for fighting depression and other related conditions. There are three basic principles that must take root before one can give service to their fullest capacity: 1) Love 2) Forgiveness 3) Gratitude.

When I started choosing life again, I decided my challenges were an opportunity to inspire and help others, so I presented speeches at schools and businesses and wrote my story for a book. These activities served the community and gave me purpose.

Laugh. We all need to be let out for recess every now and then to climb the jungle gym, skip rope, and forget about daily worries and fears. I'm convinced that making light of the situation will not solve it, but it can help you through it.

In September (2017), my wife and I attended a Boise State football game. At half time, my wife carried me from the stands to my wheelchair—except my wheelchair wasn't there; it had been stolen! I don't know who steals a wheelchair from a quadriplegic, but we had a good laugh imagining the thief and the scenario. The other funny part was that we had just spent the summer on a 1,200-mile biking event to raise money to provide wheelchairs for those in need! I wondered if the organization would loan me a chair if I needed it. No, the theft wasn't funny, but yes, we had a good laugh. A smile and a laugh go farther than a frown and a whine any day.

Touch. Touching someone you love actually reduces pain. When we don't feel loved and accepted from others, it is painful. Not disappointment, but actual pain. If you have experienced this before, you know it can hurt as much as a broken bone. Touch is more than something we crave; it is something we need. It is hard for people to hug me; I sit low to the ground and my situation makes people uncomfortable. But I need physical touch as much as you do. Sometimes I have to ask for it, but a hug or a gentle massage makes me feel normal again. So reach out and give someone a hug, and odds are, you'll both feel better.

Therapy. There's nothing I want more than to feel like a normal guy, not like someone who has to ask for help for everything. I didn't want to admit I needed help, much less ask for it. Which is why I didn't. It was because of my wife that I ended up going to therapy, and only then because I wanted to support her, not because I thought I truly needed it. But therapy has changed my life. To this day, the therapist remains a good friend, and I have an actual plan for conquering depression and making steps toward my goals.

PERFECT AND IMPERFECT

The paradox of paralysis is that the same scenario that causes me so much pain and frustration also creates gifts and blessings. Spending untold hours in a wheelchair forced me to slow down—

and taught me to appreciate the present. I learned to stop rushing into the next activity and find the joy and happiness in each moment. I taught my young children about how bees pollinate flowers and why airplanes fly in the sky—because I was forced to stop and take it all in. Many of those little opportunities get lost if we get too busy or demand too much of ourselves.

The four wheels that became my new limbs indeed push me to look at life from a new viewpoint.

Bridging the Gap

The gap—between the perfect picture of my life and my reality—will always be there. But I know the misery doesn't have to accompany it. Defeat is certain, but misery is optional.

The bridge that now crosses the divide between life as I imagined it and life as I live it was built one beam at a time. Every inch of beam represents a goal met, even when the goal was as simple as taking a shower. In the beginning especially, it was not the goal itself, but simply having finish lines to work toward that kept pushing me. Perhaps the most important part of the construction process was just that I kept building.

The Road to Higher Ground

In the last few years, I've welcomed the return of confidence and determination and invited them to settle in for the long haul. I've taken on new challenges: snow skiing, snorkeling, skydiving, a half-triathlon, and rappelling off a 150-foot cliff in southern Utah. I'm not telling you it is easy; you may still experience days in the abyss. But when you fight to loosen the grip of depression, you are free to climb again. The rocky road of depression gives us the opportunity to reach great heights in the future. Climb on!

Ignite the Strength—Heather's Story

It's strange that a single moment can change the direction of your life, but when I found out that Nate broke his neck, it upended all of our goals and sent the world spinning.

With little choice, I sprinted into survival mode. Holding my husband's hand while he lay on a bed in the E.R., I smiled for a camera, wondering if the photo would be our last together. The drone in me stayed in high gear, signing papers, talking to the doctors, and nodding at every risk and potential disaster thrown at me. But I didn't fall prey to a catastrophe mindset. With Nate temporarily out of the picture as a parent and provider, I knew I had two little kids who needed stability.

My children and I stayed at my parents' house while Nate fought for his life. That first night, I tried to nurse our eleven-month-old son, Kyler, as though everything were normal. But within the first day or two, my milk completely dried up. The body knows how to adapt. Mine signaled that our family was going to change—the baby phase had ended and the time had come for me to take care of my husband.

After tucking the kids in, I collapsed onto the bed in my old room. My mind played endless videos from the day, and I knew I couldn't endure the dark night alone. I dragged myself into my parents' room, crawled into bed, and sobbed. All my pent-up emotions and worries spilled out: Who was going to make money? Who was going to provide? Was I someone who could lead out to take care of my family?

Even at twenty-four years old with two children, I felt somehow comforted as I curled on the bed and let them take care of me.

Choosing Sides for the Fight

Fast forward a few days. Two distinct sides appeared, like rivals at a game. One team cried endless tears and talked as though Nate was never getting better. The other team cheered us on and held onto hope. I quickly learned I needed to be on the right side, with the positive and encouraging supporters. I needed boundaries, like markers on a field, to guide me, to keep myself safe (from the negativity of others). We needed to focus on the end goal of Nathan living and healing; we could not entertain thoughts about the *what ifs* still in play.

The *what if* happened in my life—and it changed everything in an instant. There was nothing I could do to stop it, but I did get to choose whether I let it rule our lives or push us forward. I chose to push Nathan to the fastest recovery possible and not to waste my strength worrying about what else could happen.

But the divide pushed on. People around us chose sides; The Naysayers wanted to coddle and enable him; they played the handicapped card and said we should move out of our home, get him full-time care, and I should give up our plans for the future.

The Believers—and I—wanted to push Nate. We knew if he started in an electric wheelchair, a joystick chair, he'd never get out. We lost so much in the accident; I didn't want to lose independence, too.

Giving in to the Naysayers forecast felt like forfeiting the game before we'd even begun. I felt strongly that my primary purpose was to help Nate think, "I am going to get better."

DARK TIMES

I won't lie and say our version of the game of life has been easy. If anything, just when we started to climb the scoreboard, the defense pushed us back. But we kept playing, through hospitalizations, surgeries, and almost unbelievably, a second neck break.

Miraculously, all of that didn't drive me into the darkness of depression. But when a drunk driver hit our car, our world crashed with it. That accident left *me* with brain trauma. I withered to ninety-eight pounds, and Nate started to look like a skeleton. When I was sidelined, we realized how much he depended on me; his health and weight fell, fast.

One night he didn't have a shirt on and I could see his ribs and concave chest. In my mind, I heard a voice; it spoke to me and said, "If [Nathan] does not turn around his health, he will not be here by the holidays." This was October.

He was wrestling with a terrible bout of depression, but *I couldn't help him*. I had a brain injury; I couldn't remember, read, or put words together. I slept all the time and drank Ensure as food.

I was trying to get me better, but there was no way I could save both of us. Indeed, the darkest time came with the most clarity.

Preparing to Care

Like it or not, I had to take care of myself or face the prospect that our family could lose both of us. All I could do was pray that my husband would do something more to take care of himself.

For me, it meant learning to take care of myself before giving my all to others. I had to figure out how to start with enough energy, and then expend it in the right ways so I could last through the whole game.

I don't have a lot of specifics of how I handled life and my own dark times; I just have a few, but I know the importance of them.

Take time for yourself. Even in the throws of a huge catastrophe, you have time, even if it a fifteen-minute nap or twenty minutes for prayer. There is time. I have to make sure I have enough sleep. I cannot help others if I am on my last straw because I haven't slept. Make yourself a priority.

Let it go. Realize that not every dinner has to be homemade and not every event has to be Pinterest-worthy. Let some things go, but know which things you CAN'T let go because they are important to you. I enjoy homemade meals and I will make them if I have time, but in a pinch, even a bag of peanuts will do.

Keep your environment clean and uncluttered. When we didn't come home after Nate's accident, others came into our home to get our belongings and take down our Christmas tree. From that time on, I knew that I never wanted anyone having to come in to clean up our mess. And when my surroundings are a mess, I feel like life is a mess. Keep up with the basics so you can control your surroundings and your surroundings don't control you.

Ditch the rating scale. I don't have any rating scale for catastrophes and challenges. The Ogden family struggles may seem harder than some others, but our challenges are all the same to me as a divorce, losing a child, or being out of work for a year. Everyone has trials that are hard for them. There is no point in comparing to others.

Voice your situation. Rather than trying to rank how bad your situation is, give it a voice. Try to say, "I'm struggling," or "this is challenging me." It gives you power and helps you recognize that what you are going through is real. Anytime I can capture my feelings, I voice them; I let them out and it frees me to deal with them instead of hiding them.

Rely on God. With God, we can do this and whatever else may come. Challenges are just situations we haven't learned to handle YET. But we need to recognize *who* teaches us how to handle the hardships. We can heal from any ailment when we trust the great Physician. I feel like God prepared me for this life. My older sister had special needs, and later I had friends and roommates whom I cared for. Now I see that He started healing me before some of the wounds were struck.

Do what you can. We have gone to counselors and tried therapies, and they help. But sometimes we don't realize that many of the abilities and answers we need are already within us. We just need to ignite them. What better way to start a fire than with the flame of a trial? Do what you can. Live now so you can prepare yourself for whatever is to come.

THE HINGE

Maybe an eternal optimist lives inside me, but I truly believe that the outcome of my life hinges on my attitude far more than on my circumstances. Time and time again, I have to choose whether to side with the Force or let the Dark Side win. But deep down, *I know that Nate can get better*, even though he will never walk again.

What have I learned? Life may not be there tomorrow. Live in THIS moment. Laugh, smile, and choose joy, and you'll always be enough for yourself and the ones you love.

PRESS ON.

RISE.

Epilogue

by Jodi Orgill Brown

"When you keep searching for ways to change your situation for the better, you stand a chance of finding them. When you stop searching, assuming they can't be found, you guarantee they won't."   --
Angela Duckworth, Author of Grit

No matter where you are in the fight with depression, promise yourself, and your loved ones, that you will never stop searching for solutions. You *can* embrace love and peace by experiencing the in-the-moment ebbs and flows of life. Low tide comes with a promise that high tide is on the way.

Take the picture-perfect painting you have for your life off the wall and turn it upside down. Remind yourself that Superman is a comic book figure and Barbie is a doll. Real beauty, and beautiful lives, comes from a willingness to experience the messiness of life.

Rising above does not promise an end to pain or sadness, but it is a path to new perspective through perseverance.

It is time. Start, or continue, your escalation out of the darkness. Leave the mire below and elevate yourself.

PRESS ON.

RISE.

BONUS! Download FREE happiness guide at: http://bit.ly/riseabovedepression

Acknowledgements

The last several years have shown me how any anguish, hurt, fear, or wrong of man can be righted by God's infinite power. I've benefited from and seen that every person can be an angel to someone else if they act when the thought comes. All experiences, even the most difficult, can be for our good, if we press on and keep faith when times are tough.

A complete list of acknowledgments would be nearly impossible to compile. However, I would like to make special reference to a few individuals, without whom I would not be the person I am, nor would I be able to complete projects such as this one.

My husband, Tolan, is the most supportive force in my life. He forgives easily when I screw up and encourages easily, even when I feel inadequate. He loves to learn best practices, implement them into his life, and then share his knowledge with his family; I have been fortunate enough to pick up a few of his habits along the way. Tolan is solid, steady, and sure, as a life partner and eternal companion. He forever holds my hand and heart.

The four children I was blessed to bring into this world are the most self-sufficient young people I know. Trenden, Lindi, Casen, and Daven have taken family hardships and turned them into personal strengths, for which I am forever in awe and in love with them. I never knew I would give birth to my best friends. They inspire me and make me want to become a better person.

My parents, Von and Sherri K. Orgill, continue to be forces for good in my life, but more importantly, in the world around them. They are father and mother to hundreds, if not thousands; however, I am one of a privileged few to have been born into their parentage. They occupy a seat at every performance and read every page I write. They continue to amaze me with their love and their selfless service and sacrifice.

Thanks to all the authors, contributors, and individuals who added to this project and who believed in me, especially: Angie Fenimore, Celeste Noland, Kristy Jo Hunt, Nathan and Heather Ogden, Tamara Heiner, Andee Sanders, and Jessica Thornton.

About The Author & Editor

Jodi Orgill Brown is the author of the multiple award-winning book and Amazon bestseller, *The Sun Still Shines*, a memoir of her fight for life with a brain tumor. She lives in Utah with her husband, Tolan, and their four children. Jodi is inspired by God's creations and people who live fulfilled lives in spite of their struggles.

She received a Master of Science degree in organizational communication from the University of Utah, a Bachelor of Arts degree in public relations from Brigham Young University, and is a Certified Fund Raising Executive (CFRE) and nonprofit consultant.

Jodi has lived on both U.S. coasts and studied in Israel, but knows home is wherever her family is.

Connect with Jodi

www.writerjodibrown.com
Email: jodi@jodiobrown.com
Facebook: www.facebook.com/jodiobrown
Instagram: jodiorgillbrown

Purchase Jodi's memoir, *The Sun Still Shines*, at Amazon.com.

Please Leave a Review

If you found this book useful, please post a review on Amazon or Goodreads. All reviews are read, and feedback will be used to improve future versions of this book.

Download FREE happiness guide at:
http://bit.ly/riseabovedepression

AUTHOR CONTRIBUTORS

Angie Fenimore is an international bestselling author and writing coach. Find her online at www.angiefenimore.com.

Blen W. Harline is an amateur writer, a Christian singer/songwriter, father, husband, and a U.S. Soldier.

Brandon T. Orgill is a writer with an eclectic assortment of experiences, skills, and expectations. Find him at www.abucketofrandomness.blogspot.com.

Camille Ballou works as a CPA, spends her free time volunteering for the local FFA chapter, and hangs out with her family and their beloved Labrador.

Christy Monson is a retired Marriage and Family Therapist who has written several books on living well. www.christymonson.com.

Dyany Munson is a peer support specialist, speaker, and aspiring author. Find her online at www.dyany.com.

Janet M. Bernice, MA, is a writer and an online college instructor.

Jeni Farner is a writer for Grace Lane Authors. Read more of her experiences at www.gracelaneauthors.com.

Jessica Thornton is an undergraduate student at the University of South Florida majoring in creative writing and advertising.

Julianne Kelsch is a professional development expert trained in the art of communication. She is also an author and a mother. Find her online at www.juliannekelsch.com.

Kate Durtschi earned a BA in English from BYU and is an Army veteran, a wife, a mother of four, and a writer.

Keri Montgomery is a writer, a board member for the League of Utah Writers, and president of the Brigham City Writers chapter. Find her on Twitter @kerigmont and at brighamcitywriters.blogspot.com.

Kristy Jo Hunt is a Mind and Body Strategist who specializes in Women's Autoimmune Conditions and Emotional Eating Recovery. Find her online at PowerFoodsLifestyle.com

Lori Conger is a mother, wife, speaker, and survivor of the Cokeville Elementary hostage crisis. Learn more about Lori by visiting her blog, loriconger.blogspot.com.

Nathan and Heather Ogden are parents and authors, and both are brain injury survivors. Visit their website www.nathanogden.com.

Paul H. Jenkins, Ph.D. is a speaker, author, and personal development coach. He is The Positivity Psychologist. Learn more at www.drpauljenkins.com.

Rebecca Clayson is a wife, mother, aspiring author, prolific reader, Snoopy groupie, and chocolate connoisseur. For more, visit her blog at rebeccajclayson.blogspot.com.

CONTRIBUTORS

Alesia Budd

Amy Furr

Andrea Lofthaus

Angie Fenimore

Aubrey Loose

Brandon T. Orgill

Blen Harline

Brandi Nicole Astle

Camille Ballou

Celeste Noland

Chris Finch

Christine Cottle

Christy Monson

Debbie Kidd

Dyany Munson

Erin Grimley

Fika Mariana

Heidi Robbins Tighe

Jamie Neff

Janet Bernice

Jeremy Gohier

John Marler

Julianne Kelsch

Karen Gillespie Hoover

Kara Forsyth Cottle

Karen Johnson

Kate Durtschi

Kathryn Ann Olsen

Kathy Wade

Kelly Parkinson

Kendra Miller

Kristy Jo Hunt

Laurie Richards

LeAnn Emery

Lori Conger

Maline Nath

Michelle Poll

Nathan Croft

Nathan Ogden

Paul Jenkins

Peter Duggen

Phil Ritzert

Rachel Decker Bolin

Randi Spicer

Rebecca Clayson

Richie Norton

Robin Cranney

Sabrina J. Watts

Sadee Carney

Sandi Rytting

Tawni Weston

Tami O. Baker

Tammy Warren

Appendix

TYPES OF TREATMENT THERAPY
by Jessica Thornton

Generally, when people think of therapy, they think of the kind they are used to seeing on television and in movies. They envision a stuffy room with framed certificates hanging on the walls while an uncomfortable patient responds to a therapist asking, "And how does that make you feel?"

The good news is, if that doesn't sound like ideal treatment for your depression, it's likely not the kind of treatment you will receive. There are many different kinds of therapy that can help with depression, so you can find one that works best for you.

Cognitive Behavioral Therapy, or CBT, is the therapy most familiar to the media, although it is not quite like the TV tropes. CBT aims to adjust your undesired or unhealthy patterns of thoughts or behavior to healthier or more positive alternatives. While engaging in this type of therapy, you are more likely to discuss your current status (hence, the cliché of "How does that make you feel?") than events from earlier times in your life. It is usually a one-on-one situation between you and a therapist, but can also include your family or possibly a group scenario.

Since the aim of CBT is often to explore and understand the mental health status of the patient as well as to suggest coping mechanisms and the like, your first session will be for your therapist to gain a general overview of these things. When attending your first CBT session, you can expect discussions surrounding what you are interested in exploring through therapy. During the discussions at your first session, your therapist will also try to determine what kind of therapy will work best for you and the duration and frequency of your meetings. The steps of CBT often include identifying the negative impacts in your life, both internal and external, and reforming your thoughts and approaches to those negative sources so they affect you less.

Generally speaking, CBT is a short-term type of therapy, usually lasting between ten and twenty meetings. However, throughout your meetings, the intensity of your mental health conditions can be a determining factor of how many meetings are necessary. One way to get the most out of your CBT meetings is to ensure that you have a good, comfortable relationship with your therapist. This is another aspect that can be determined at the first few meetings, if not the first. Finding another therapist is always an option that can help you progress in your recovery process.

CBT, like all kinds of therapy, does aim to help you on an emotional and mental level, but your therapist will ease you into talking about those things, should you feel apprehension about those topics. If you do not feel like you are being eased into those topics or will be able to ease into those topics with your particular therapist, again, finding another therapist is always an option.[xxi]

Neuro-Linguistic Programming, or NLP, is an option. This type of therapy is based on the theory that everyone understands and interacts with the world differently because everyone's experiences shape their minds in different ways. It is difficult for us to have access to exactly how those experiences have shaped our minds, our main channel into that interaction being our emotions and behavior. NLP aims to examine a patient's emotions and behaviors so as to understand the neurological reasoning that led to them. Your personal experiences will have shaped your brain's reactions to positive and negative influences differently than the way anyone else's experiences will shape theirs. NLP therapy understands this and uses it as the basis of treatment to helping your specific mental health status.[xxii]

Eye movement therapy, or EMDR, was originally developed for sufferers of post-traumatic stress disorder and eventually was found to be helpful in cases of depression as well. EMDR works especially well in cases wherein a person's depression is mainly caused or triggered by a certain trauma or event. Through this type of treatment, that trauma or trigger is desensitized so it will not affect the depressed individual as much or, hopefully and ultimately, at all. The goal in the end is to be less affected by the event, not to erase it entirely from one's memory. This therapy, much like other types of therapy, does not immediately throw you into the treatment all at once. It will begin with establishing a trusting and open relationship with a therapist for several meetings before the eye movement therapy begins. [xxiii]

Group therapy is yet another option of depression treatment. Since depression is a more common problem than you may think, group therapy is a viable therapy option. This type of therapy can be especially beneficial in helping alleviate the notion that you are alone in the way you feel. Group therapy can help you feel less alone as well as learn about other people's coping mechanisms. Although not everyone's coping mechanisms will work for you, there is a good chance a couple will work for you, too, which is certainly an advantage to group therapy.

If going to therapy alone sounds uncomfortable, as does a group setting, family therapy is also available. This kind of therapy is generally useful with children or adolescents, but even if you are older than that, family therapy can be an option, too.

Psychotherapy deals more with past or childhood events and how they influence you today. These influences can manifest in a number of ways, including depression. This type of therapy might be worth trying out if you think working through past issues will help your current depression or if you have already tried another kind of therapy and the past keeps cropping up in your discussions.

Mindfulness is often used to target problems such as depression, anxiety, or stress by honing in on specific tactics, including meditation or other breathing exercises, with the goal of easing your thoughts, emotions, or impulses without overtly focusing on or discussing them. Mindfulness-based therapy can be a great way to find coping mechanisms for your depression.

Interpersonal therapy can be helpful if you are having difficulty with interpersonal relationships because of depression. Managing depression while maintaining relationships with friends and family can be difficult, but even more so if you have difficulty identifying problems within those relationships because of your depression.

If you try one and find it truly is not for you, trying another option can still be beneficial to you. One thing all of these types of therapy have in common is that they all ensure confidentiality between the therapist and patient. Save a few extreme circumstances in which your therapist is under the impression that people are in danger, nothing you say in any therapy session will be repeated elsewhere by your therapist. Your best interest is always kept in mind, regardless of the type of therapy.

WORKS CITED

"14 Homeopathic Remedies for Depression - Natural Treatment Depression." Daily Free Health Articles and Natural Health Advice. N.p., 05 May 2016. Web. 30 Mar. 2017. http://www.doctorshealthpress.com/brain-function-articles/homeopathic-remedies-for-depression

"About Us." American Art Therapy Association. N.p., n.d. Web. 25 Mar. 2017. http://arttherapy.org/aata-aboutus/

"American Music Therapy Association." FAQ's | Frequently Asked Questions | American Music Therapy Association (AMTA). N.p., n.d. Web. 25 Mar. 2017. http://www.musictherapy.org/faq/#39

"About Horticultural Therapy." American Horticultural Therapy Association. N.p., n.d. Web. 25 Mar. 2017. http://www.ahta.org/horticultural-therapy

"Eye Movement Therapy (EMDR) for Depression." EverydayHealth.com. N.p., 03 May 2010. Web. 30 Mar. 2017. http://www.everydayhealth.com/depression/eye-movement-therapy-for-depression.aspx

"FAQs." ADTA. N.p., n.d. Web. 25 Mar. 2017. https://adta.org/faqs/

"Major Depressive Disorder." Springer Reference (n.d.): n. pag. Web. http://images.pearsonclinical.com/images/assets/basc-3/basc3resources/DSM5_DiagnosticCriteria_MajorDepressiveDisorder.pdf

"Neuro-Linguistic Programming." Good Therapy. N.p., n.d. Web. 30 Mar. 2017. http://www.goodtherapy.org/learn-about-therapy/types/neuro-linguistic-programming

"Talking Therapies Explained - Stress, Anxiety and Depression." NHS Choices. NHS, n.d. Web. 25 Mar. 2017. http://www.nhs.uk/Conditions/ stress-anxiety-depression/Pages/Types-of-therapy.aspx

"The Effects of Depression on the Brain." Healthline. N.p., n.d. Web. 25 Mar. 2017. http://www.healthline.com/health/depression/effects-brain#2

http://www.mayoclinic.org/tests-procedures/cognitive-behavioral-therapy/details/what-you-can-expect/rec-20188674

http://www.ncbi.nlm.nih.gov/pmc/articles/PMC3150158/

http://psychcentral.com/lib/social-support-is-critical-for-depression-recovery/00010852

FOOTNOTES

i http://www.healthline.com/health/depression/causes#overview1

ii https://www.health.harvard.edu/mind-and-mood/what-causes-depression

iii http://www.monologuearchive.com/s/shakespeare_001.html

iv http://www.healthline.com/health/depression/effects-brain#2

v Dr. Celeste Campbell, neuropsychologist, Washington DC Veterans Administration Medical Center

vi http://sethgodin.typepad.com/seths_blog/2017/10/thepleasurehappiness-gap.html

vii http://sethgodin.typepad.com/seths_blog/2017/10/thepleasurehappiness-gap.html

viii http://sethgodin.typepad.com/seths_blog/2017/10/thepleasurehappiness-gap.html

ix http://time.com/4070299/secret-to-happiness/

x http://www.deseretnews.com/article/865687782/God-did-not-do-this-to-us-LDS-couple-shares-messages-of-hope-on-social-media-after-son-hit-by-SUV.html

xi RCMS 2010 religious congregations census

xii https://imhcn.org/bibliography/life-domains/education-and-skills/

xiii https://psychcentral.com/blog/archives/2009/07/09/6-steps-for-beating-depression/

xi "Everything You Think You Know About Addiction is Wrong", Johann Hari, TED Talks, July 2015. https://youtu.be/PY9DcIMGxMs

xiii http://www.apa.org/monitor/2011/06/social-networking.aspx

xiv "Sir Duke", composed and performed by Stevie Wonder.

xv Saarman, Emily. "Feeling the Beat: Symposium Explores the Therapeutic Effects of Rhythmic Music." Stanford University. N.p., 31 May 2006. Web. 09 Feb. 2017.

xvi http://bjp.rcpsych.org/content/199/2/92

xvii http://owaves.com/day-plans/michael-phelps/

xx http://www.businessinsider.com/arnold-palmer-quotes-2016-9

xxi http://www.mayoclinic.org/tests-procedures/cognitive-behavioral-therapy/details/what-you-can-expect/rec-20188674 xxii http://www.goodtherapy.org/learn-about-therapy/types/neuro-linguistic-programming

xxi http://www.everydayhealth.com/depression/eye-movement-therapy-for-depression.aspx

Made in the USA
Columbia, SC
30 July 2021

42466289R00139